Seven Saved Sinners
or How God Saves Men

---

*A Study of God's Varieties of Religious Experience
in the Book of Acts*

By

William Ward Ayer, D.D.,

Pastor of Calvary Baptist Church, New York City

ZONDERVAN PUBLISHING HOUSE
GRAND RAPIDS, MICHIGAN

EIGHT-FIFTEEN FRANKLIN STREET
GRAND RAPIDS, MICHIGAN

To Lucile, a Companion and Co-Worker
in a Blessed Soul-Winning Ministry.

INTRODUCTION

In 1902, Professor William James of Harvard University delivered the Gifford Lectures on natural religion at the University of Edinburgh. The general topic was "The Varieties of Religious Experience."

Psychology, thirty-five years ago, was vastly more immature than today; but even then it was setting itself up as an interpretative science. Human emotions and human actions were being probed, dissected and analyzed with the idea of discovering the origins of human conduct. The psychology of religion has made for the exploration of a vast field of human emotion and conduct. No sane person, especially no devout person, can agree with all the conclusions of this growing science. Yet, where the spirit has been reverent, it is discovered that much valuable material has been mined for the use of those who work in the realm of the Christian religion.

Professor James' book was doubtless considered basic in the study of religious psychology, and although he could never have been called evangelical, nevertheless he provided a great deal of material which can be used by evangelicals. Harold Begbie, in the early years of the century, wrote his book, *Twice-Born Men*. He said he wrote it as a foot-note to Professor James' monumental work. You will remember that *Twice-Born Men* tells the story of a group of most unusual conversions effected through the work of the Salvation Army in England. Begbie based his book on the statement of Professor James, in which he says that in true conversion men and women who previously were "consciously wrong, consciously inferior and consciously unhappy" were transformed to a condition of being "consciously right, consciously superior, and consciously happy."

Now a careful study of that great book on evangelism, *The Acts of the Apostles*, will reveal that there are just seven individual conversions recorded. The study of these conversions shows that they are typical conversions, and that they doubtless present *God's varieties of religious experience*. Each one portrays a distinctly different human condition, and in most cases a different emotional accompaniment. The results, from the human standpoint, often differ widely, but in every case it is the saving Gospel which brings about the change in the life, and evidences in every case the ability of an all-wise and an all-powerful God to meet human need.

As we give these pages to the public we have a twofold purpose in mind which will easily be seen as the book is perused. In each case we have given a brief semi-technical study of the conversion and its results under the following headings: 1. The Occasion; 2. The Subject; 3. The Agent; 4. The Accompaniment; 5. The Result; 6. Significant Lessons. Then follows the sermon on the theme.

These sermons do not follow the outlines of the technical study, but those adapted to appeal to the hearts of listeners. The messages have been preached in four localities and in two countries, and broadcast over four different radio stations in the United States and Canada. In almost every case when these messages were presented, souls found Christ as their Saviour; and we have discovered that in the presentation of these varieties of religious experience, others were encouraged to find God in Christ and their own blessed conversion experience.

We would not be dogmatic about the matter, but we feel after much study of these conversions that they are typical, and universal in their typicalness; that is, that practically every conversion could be grouped, in a general way, under the experience of one of these conversions found in *The Book of Acts.* These are God's varieties of religious experience.

In a careful study of these seven religious experiences we note the following facts:

1. Six of the seven converts recorded were men.

2. Previous preparation of one kind or another is evident in almost every instance. There is only one apparent "immediate" conversion of "raw" soul. Note, further, these facts: (a) The Eunuch was doubtless a Jewish proselyte, before Philip led him to Christ. (b) Saul, though rebellious, was well trained in the Scriptures. (c) Cornelius was a religious man with some knowledge of, and faith in, Jehovah. (d) Sergius Paulus' preparation seems to have been of an adverse nature through Elymas, the false prophet. Yet he was in a religious frame of mind when the apostles approached him with the Gospel. (e) Lydia was a devout Gentile, probably a Jewish proselyte, whose heart God had visited in a preparatory way. (f) The Philippian jailer may be the one exception to the rule. If we are to consider his question, "What must I do to be saved?"

a non-religious one—which we believe it was—there is little evidence of any previous knowledge of the Gospel or of the true God. (g) Apollos was a half-Christian when he came to Ephesus, being trained in religion and the Scriptures in the city of Alexandria, in Egypt.

3. How widely differentiated are the emotional accompaniments of these conversions! If we divide them into two general classes, "calm" and "hilarious," we would place the Eunuch, Sergius Paulus, Lydia and Apollos in the first group; and Saul, Cornelius and the Philippian jailer in the second.

4. The outward accompaniments of the experiences could be divided into classifications of "quiet" and "uproarious." These classifications reveal the Eunuch, Cornelius, Lydia and Apollos as "quiet" conversions; Saul, Sergius Paulus and the Philippian jailer as "uproarious." It is plain that according to God's varieties of religious experience, the "quiet" and "calm" predominate, while the "hilarious" and the "uproarious" may be expected on occasion.

5. The genuineness of conversion is attested in the Scriptures by either rejoicing of heart, as the case of the Eunuch, or resultant good works, of which Lydia is an example; or both, as in the case of the Philippian jailer and Apollos. Sergius Paulus stands without comment in his reaction to belief, and we know nothing more of his life. Conclusions which may be reached concerning our soul-saving ministries in the analysis of these conversions embrace the following facts: (1) The majority of our converts must be *prepared* for that experience. (2) We must expect wide divergence

of human reaction to the same saving truth, and much variation in the outward accompaniments of conversion. (3) God is a God of variety. (4) We have a right to expect evidence of genuineness in manifested joy and new life motives in every true Christian conversion.

CONTENTS

I.

THE CONVERSION OF THE ETHIOPIAN EUNUCH

Acts 8: 26-39.

THE STUDY

The Occasion.

WE HAVE here an apparently incidental meeting of
Philip the Evangelist and this Eunuch of Ethiopia. Yet
study reveals that there was a divine preparation made
with both individuals of this important meeting. *There
are no coincidences with God.* God is a God of plan
and of purpose. In the study of the experience the un-
usualness of the situation must be kept in mind to appreciate the results. The prominence and dignity of
the Eunuch is contrasted with the obscurity and boldness of the messenger, Philip. The story is so well
known as not to need further comment.

The Subject.

The Eunuch was the Secretary of the Treasury of
Queen Candace of Ethiopia; a man of renown and influence, a man who evidently often visited Jerusalem,
and appears to have been a proselyte to the Jewish faith
but is not born again through faith in our Lord Jesus
Christ. He is an earnest seeker after truth.

The Agent.

Philip, the evangelist, was one of the seven deacons of the primitive Church of Jerusalem (Acts 6: 1-6). When the Christians, except the apostles, were driven from Jerusalem by the persecution after Stephen's death, Philip went to Samaria, where he preached the Gospel with great success and wrought many miracles. You will remember his conflict with Simon, recorded in Acts 8: 1-13. From the busy revival of the populous Samaritan city, Philip was divinely led into a lonely spot, and on one of the roads between Jerusalem and Gaza he finds this Ethiopian Eunuch. Now he is rather a peculiar agent for such a task, ordinarily we deem it best for personal work to be done by "like with like"; and Philip would appear, humanly speaking, to be the most unlikely agent for such a task; but God does not always follow human rules and here at least He has done a most remarkable thing with individuals who are contrasts in personality.

The Accompaniments.

As we look at this conversion we discover that the whole process here is a quiet, undisturbed one. There is no apparent opposition of man or devil. Philip, in some unexplained way, is able to approach the chariot, mount it and, sitting beside the great Treasurer from Ethiopia, is able to explain the Scriptures to a heart that is seeking truth, and then there is the quiet acceptance of it followed by the baptism of the convert. Here we have a type of "intellectual" conversion, if we may use such a term; but as is true with every conversion of this type, the heart is touched and the life changed. We find a hungry heart. We find a Biblically awakened conscience. The reason we call this an intellectual conversion is because there is no apparent conviction for individual sin but rather an awakening of the mind and heart to the need of a Saviour, and a troubled mind over inability to understand the Scripture concerning the prophecy of the Messiah. The student of conversion processes will do well to note the thoroughness of Philip and to use this same thoroughness in committing inquirers to the Lord Jesus Christ.

The Result.

Briefly, Philip's mission resulted in a saved, baptized and rejoicing convert. Tradition also has it that he led his queen, Candace, to a saving knowledge of the Gospel and started a church in Ethiopia. This, of course, is not verified in reliable history.

Significant Lessons.

Two important modes of procedure stand out for the personal soul winner in this event. First, *Obedience*, which has as its prerequisite soul-contact with God, in order that His will may be known, and His directive purposes understood and followed. The true soul winner is an obedient servant of God, spiritually sensitive to the promptings of the Spirit. Second, *Tact.* Philip's approach is made relatively easy by the Eunuch's condition. Yet he should be commended for beginning his conversation with a challenging question,

"Understandest thou what thou readest?" By that question he probed the very heart of the Eunuch's spiritual difficulty. His reply shows this very definitely. It is apparent that Philip did not belong to the modern school of critics who attribute the meaning of the prophecy of Isaiah 53 to Israel's suffering as a nation, and take away its Messianic character. Without theological argument, without explanation, Philip did the commendable thing, he began at the same Scripture and preached unto the Ethiopian Eunuch, Jesus. This Christo-centric attitude is necessary for all successful soul-winners. Taboo all arguments. Exalt Jesus Christ as Saviour and Lord.

THE SERMON

"WHO IS A CHRISTIAN?"

Acts 8: 26-39.

As WE have already noted, there are just seven individual conversions recorded in *The Book of Acts*. These, as we have noted also, are seven types of conversions. Each portrays a distinctly different human condition and the ability of an all-wise and all-powerful God to meet human needs. The eighth chapter of the book records the conversion of the Ethiopian Eunuch who was a puzzled reader of the Scriptures, and to whom the Lord sent Philip, evangelist, in order that he might begin at the same Scripture and preach unto him, Jesus. Now Philip was not a minister in the commonly accepted understanding of the term; that is

to say, he was not an ordained man, but a layman. We
learn from the text that he was on speaking terms with
angels and therefore could be used of God in this
mighty task. Oh, for more laymen in our own day who
are on speaking terms with angels, and in such spiritual condition as makes it possible for God to use them
in the saving of souls!

However, some of our outstanding soul-winners
have been laymen and D. L. Moody is the supreme
example of this truth. A tendency to leave this matter
to the clergy, so called, has been one of the most detri-
mental attitudes of the Church in our day. God's program is for the entire Church to be active in the business of soul-winning and for the minister to be the
one who edifies the Church to this ministry. In an
issue of *The Sunday School Times* some years ago,
William Ridgeway tells of a common steel worker—a
roller in the mills in a Pennsylvania town—who was
so proficient in the Word of God and in prayer that
he astounded a great minister from the East who came
to Mr. Ridgeway's little Sunday School to speak. Yet
no one should be astounded. God is no respecter of
persons. A steel worker may be endued with the Spirit
and he may know the Word and be proficient in it.
God cares nothing for religious orders, the clergy are
nothing to him as an order, He deals with men as individuals.

There had been persecution in Jerusalem and the
disciples had been scattered abroad and had gone from
Judaea to Samaria, where a great revival was started.

In the midst of this revival God called Philip to go
down to Gaza, a desert place. Now you talk about
faith and obedience. Well, you have it manifested here.
It is easy to get a sinner away from a revival, but
think of getting a preacher away from such a stir-up,
such an outpouring of God's Spirit. But Philip's chief
characteristic is obedience and obedience is an essential virtue of the minister of God. When you stop and
think of it you will realize that only those who are
obedient to God are those whom God can lead and use.
Do today's plain duty and tomorrow's duty will be
made plain when it becomes to-day's. God's will is
not known very far in advance in most instances. We
sail down the river of life and we do not see around
the bend until we get around it; but if we follow the
will of God there are blessed vistas of service, purpose
and joy for us in the following.

Philip was obedient. Down there in the desert place
was a hungry heart of an important man in the eyes
of the world, a man in whom God was interested and
Philip found him riding in his chariot, reading the
scroll of the prophet Isaiah, and the dramatic story
of whose conversion will now occupy our attention.
This first conversion is worthy of study in the light of
the answer to the question, "Who is a Christian?" We
note, therefore, the following facts:

I. THAT RESPECTABILITY DOES NOT MAKE ONE A CHRISTIAN.

Who was this man? He was an Ethiopian—that
race which has come so much into prominence in our

day because of the conquering of its country by the
Italians. Ethiopia is one of the oldest of nations. He
was the Secretary of the Treasury of Queen Candace;
but above all was an earnest seeker after truth, and
his case is a pitiful one when we realize that he had
been down to Jerusalem to worship, and was on his
way back without peace, without hope, or satisfaction.

The name Jerusalem means "foundation of peace"
and this Ethiopian Eunuch (probably a Jewish proselyte) had been down there, seeking peace for his own
soul. He discovered that they had religion, a plenty.
They had the Temple, the priesthood, the gorgeous ceremonies, the processions, the paraphernalia and all the
other outward accoutrements of ceremonial religion;
but sad to relate, they had no power to help this man
to know God. Remember that this was the Jerusalem
that had recently crucified the Son of God, nailing Him
to a shameful tree, in utter rejection of both His message and His person. Jesus, the Saviour had condemned
them for their lack of spirituality, calling them blind
guides and whited sepulchres.

Similar conditions are found in many places, to-
day. Oh, the froth of so many church services! What
pomp and ceremony, show and pageantry—soft lights,
lilting music, earthly glory—but where is God? Hungry
souls are entertained, harangued, or taught the latest
man-made philosophies, but the sheep look up and are
not fed! My mail is filled with pathetic letters of
people who tell me that in their communities no one
preaches the Gospel and were it not for the fact that
the message of our church went winging through

the air into their homes, they would live without any preaching of the message of Jesus Christ.

How unfavorably poor Philip, dusty with travel, must have appeared, when compared with the immaculate and cultured priests and religious leaders of Jerusalem! Yet for all that, Philip had the message of God.

A few weeks ago, riding on a Saturday night from the home of one of my parishioners, I passed two great cathedrals. Knowing the type of service, the pomp and the ceremonies of each, I knew that the multitudes could come and go and not know of God in any experimental way. Then, the Sunday following, while passing through Columbus Circle, I heard a simple, rather illiterate individual, telling in the open air to a crowd gathered about him the story of Jesus and His love, and I couldn't help but realize that God must reject the pompous and the pretentious and turn to such men as this for the proclamation of His truth. We have reached the day when men must leave the pomp and show of our great churches and get back to the Word of God and to the simplicity of faith.

We believe in a respectable religion, but we do not believe in a *religion of respectability*. Respectability is an admirable quality, a desirable thing, but it cannot save your soul. As the poet has said:

"*The boast of heraldry, the pomp of power,*
    And all that beauty, all that wealth e'er gave,
  Await alike the inevitable hour,
    The path of glory leads but to the grave."

Here, in the Treasurer of Ethiopia, we have a man in possession of all that one could ask—money, position, pomp and power. Yet his soul was starving for God. Ah, Jesus knew the truth when He said, "What shall it profit a man if he gain the whole world and lose his own soul?"

And what about you, my friend? You may be a good citizen. You may be a good husband, a good wife, a good father, you may occupy an honest place in your community, but without Jesus Christ you're lost; for respectability will never gain heaven for you.

The story has oft been told of Charlotte Elliot, who was a church member and a highly respectable young woman. When in an evangelistic campaign someone spoke to her about her need of Jesus Christ, she was highly indignant. Was she not a moral person? Was she not a respected young lady? What need had she of this gospel which she felt applied only to the down and out; those in the lower stratum of society? But, one day, God took hold of her soul; one day, she realized that with all her goodness she was lost without Christ, and that day she allowed the Lord Jesus to come into her heart and to set up His throne there. It is then, we are told, that she wrote that beautiful hymn, which has been a blessing to millions:

> *"Just as I am without one plea,*
> *But that thy blood was shed for me,*
> *And that thou biddest me come to thee,*
> *Oh, Lamb of God, I come."*

II. READING THE BIBLE DOES NOT MAKE ONE A CHRISTIAN.

Thank God for the Book. It has blessed the world. Its message has leaped the seven seas and, today, it can be read in almost every language and dialect "from Greenland's icy mountains to India's coral strand," from Tibet to Timbuctoo. It has been the comfort and sustenance of the great and the small, until many can say from their hearts as Sir Walter Scott said in his dying hour, "Bring me the Book." "What book?" asked Lockhart. "There is but one Book!" Scott replied. And truly the master of Abbottsford was right. There is but one Book for our needy souls.

The Bible has occupied a unique place in the life and thought of the nations, especially of the English-speaking race. The other day I read that General Gordon's Bible is enshrined in a costly casket of solid crystal in the jewel room of Windsor Castle. The hero of the Sudan was so faithful to his God and so devout that during the great campaigns in Africa, when a handkerchief was seen fluttering outside of his tent, all of the servants and soldiers knew that he was waiting upon his God and must not be disturbed for anything. He gave his Bible to Queen Victoria and she had it enshrined.

Now the Bible is able to make you wise unto salvation. It contains the message of salvation. Yet mere reading of it will not save you. The Bible is not an end, it is means to an end. The Jews read it, and are not saved. Christian Scientists read it, and are en-

tangled in a maze. Many infidels and skeptics read it
for the sake of argument. They, too, fail to find salvation. In one of my former pastorates I knew a man
who was a good Bible student. He knew more about
the Bible than most preachers, but he was not saved
and had no desire to be saved. He read the Bible, night
and day, for the sake of picking flaws in it and for
the sake of using it in arguments against those who
believed the truth as it is in Jesus. During my pastorate in that city the man died—died without God,
without a knowledge of the Lord Jesus Christ; yet he
knew his Bible.

Here was this Ethiopian Eunuch, riding along in
his chariot and reading a scroll of the prophet Isaiah,
troubled in heart, earnest in spirit, eager yet ignorant
—and not saved. John gives us the answer in his
Epistle as to the place of the Bible in our salvation.
Says he, "These are written that ye might believe and
that believing ye might have life through his name."
You may be saved by the belief of the Bible, but you
can never be saved by merely reading it.

III. HEARING SERMONS DOES NOT MAKE
ONE A CHRISTIAN.

Philip "began at the same scripture and preached
unto him Jesus." I remember reading some time ago
how Charles Haddon Spurgeon was accused of same-
ness in his message. When the accusation came to
him, he did not deny it, he said, "Perhaps they are
right. It is true that no matter where I take my text,
whether it be in the Old Testament or the New, I im-

mediately hit across country to Jesus Christ, and preach Him and His saving grace."

When one knows the Lord Jesus Christ, he is able to open his Bible almost anywhere and find a message concerning Him. His face and His grace shine out from every page of the Sacred Record and the preacher is able to do as did Philip of old, to "begin at the same scripture" and preach unto his hearers the Lord Jesus Christ.

Ah, preaching is a great vocation! Nothing is more disgusting to me than to see how modern churches and modernistic preachers are turning aside from the Gospel, substituting almost everything else for the message of the pulpit—movies, plays, pageants, oratorios, and in some cases dances and girl-shows—esthetic capers of lewd women.

Angels would like the job of preaching the unsearchable riches of Jesus Christ, and, wonder of wonders, God has turned this task and privilege over to men! In some instances, they are neglecting their opportunity, turning to the entertainment of people.

When a certain preacher died in a western town, his friend and brother in the ministry preached the funeral sermon. He told of the man's faithfulness to the Gospel. He reminded the people how, day after day, and ofttimes well into the night, this faithful servant of God had gone in and out among the people, warning them, comforting them, calling attention to their need of the Lord Jesus Christ, calling upon them to repent of their evil ways and to return to God for salvation.

Said he to the throng assembled, "My friends, the greatest obstacle on your road to hell has been removed." Ah, what a tribute! The faithful minister of God is not only a stumbling-block to the devil, but he is a veritable dam that stops the flowing of lost souls into perdition. I make no apology for being a preacher. Preaching is worth something to the community. It is worth something to society. It makes its contribution to social welfare, moral growth, the very preservation of society and civilization, and I declare that I covet as a preacher a similar tribute to that paid this pioneer of the west.

But for all that, listening to preaching will not save you. I know that many of you like me, know that you like my message but, sad to say, some of you refuse to conform to the truth which I present to you by the help of God. In every pastorate I have served, there have been a number who, although they listened to the truth as it was preached, Sunday after Sunday, nevertheless allowed their hearts to become sermon-hardened and, like a man who sleeps while the alarm clock rings, soon came to the place where there was no awakening their conscience or stirring their souls. They slept the sleep of death, and oh, the terribleness of going to sleep under the preaching of the truth as it is in Jesus!

And the preacher is not always to blame; some went to sleep under Paul's preaching, and Jesus preached the best sermons this old world has ever heard. They commended Him for His preaching and yet many of them are in hell for all that, because hear-

ing sermons never saved a man. Jesus was forced to
say in desperation to his generation: "You are like
children in the market place. I have piped and you
have not danced." In other words, He said, "You listen to me but you heed not my message." And I have
pleaded with you and still many of you are yet in your
sins. Oh, wake up, friends! You can go away from
a service with a religious feeling and a real desire to
do good and to be better, and yet go with that feeling
straight to perdition. For listening to sermons will not
save you; but heeding the message of the Gospel will.

IV. Believing and Receiving the Gospel Does Make One a Christian.

The Eunuch asked two questions: First, "Of whom
speaketh this man, of himself or of some other man?"
The second, "What doth hinder me to be baptized?"

Philip's answer to the first question was that the
prophet was speaking about Jesus—the Suffering Re-
deemer, the man who paid the penalty of the world's
sins in His own body on the tree, and then when the
Ethiopian believed and asked baptism at the hands of
Philip, the reply to the second question was this: "If
thou believest with all thine heart, thou mayest." The
Eunuch replied very solemnly and clearly: "I believe
that Jesus Christ is the Son of God." Here is the crux
of the whole matter. "If thou believest; if thou believest"! Take your Bible and see how many times,
especially in the New Testament, the Word of God
makes this demand of the sinner. "Whosoever believeth," "He that believeth," "If thou shalt believe."

This is the Word of God. In the world, "seeing is believing." In the realm of the Spirit, "believing is seeing."

The story is told of the conversion of Lady Somerset, a rich and fashionable woman of England. She had read a great many infidel books and her faith had been shattered. Nevertheless, she was heavyhearted, seeking to get back to her faith and to an uncompromising knowledge of God in Jesus Christ. She read and prayed and studied and yet she said she had no rest. One evening, in awful turmoil of soul while walking amid the beauty of her garden, she thought she heard a voice say, "Act as if I were, and thou shalt know that I am." Lady Somerset acted upon that suggestion, and faith came to her heart. She performed an act of trust in the simple commitment of her life to Jesus Christ and became one of England's great Christians. This, after all, is the message by which anyone becomes a Christian. "Said I not if thou shouldst believe, thou shouldst see the glory of God," is the Word of Jesus. Oh, my friend, tonight do you believe that God can save you? Do you believe that Jesus Christ died for you? Do you believe that He cares? Hear this bit of poetry:

> *"Among so many can He care?*
> *Can special love be everywhere?*
> *A myriad homes, a myriad ways—*
> *God's eye be over every place?*
>
> *I asked my soul; bethought of this—*
> *In just the very place of His*

Where He has put and keepeth you—
God hath no other thing to do."

Some years ago, out in the West, Tod Sloane, a
famous jockey, died. A former friend of his, later converted and a minister of the gospel, heard that his
old friend was in the County Hospital, penniless and
said to be dying. This young man lifted his heart to
God and asked for an open door of opportunity to
speak to Tod about his relationship to Jesus Christ.
They had both been riders for Lord Carnarvon and
King George V, when he was Prince of Wales. So early
the next morning this young minister went to the hospital and asked the head nurse if he could see Mr.
Sloane for a moment.

"I'm sorry," she answered, "but I'm afraid that
you will not be able to see him. The publicity given
him in the papers has made it very hard for us here
at the hospital. Hundreds have called, wanting to see
him, all saying that they knew him."

"Well, nurse," replied the pastor, "please go and
tell him that a pastor of a Los Angeles church would
like to speak with him just a minute."

Promptly the word came back that Sloane did not
want to see any minister. Refusing to be discouraged,
this faithful pastor said, "Go back and tell him that
an old boy he knows, who rode for Lord Carnarvon
and the Prince of Wales, would like to see him."

This broke down the barrier. Tod sent back word,
"Tell him to wait. I want to see him." Then, by
Sloane's bedside the faithful minister chatted with him,

and they reminisced together about old times. A little later, Tod asked the minister if he had anything to drink. "No, Tod," was the reply, "not the kind of drink you are looking for. I don't drink that stuff any more. I have had a drink of the Living Water that really satisfies those who drink." The dying jockey stared at his former friend. "What do you mean?" he asked.

"I mean," said the pastor, "that I was saved twenty years ago in Paterson, New Jersey, in a Billy Sunday meeting, after having lived a life somewhat like that which you have lived." The minister spoke to him of the woman at the well, of Nicodemus, and of the dying thief on the cross, and then told him how he could come to the Lord Jesus Christ just as he was, weary and worn and sad, and find in Him a resting place, and that He would make him glad.

"Tod, old boy, this is the reason Jesus left his home in glory, so that you and I might drink of the water of life," said the preacher.

The jockey looked up at his former friend with new interest in his face. "Billy Sunday came into my pool hall on Forty-second Street and Broadway, in New York, years ago, and told me I needed religion, and I said I didn't want any religion."

"Tod," said the preacher, "don't you believe that Jesus is the Son of God? Don't you believe that He not only died for the sins of the world but He hung on the Cross for your sins?" The dissipated, tired and worn out little jockey hung his head and soberly replied, "Yes, I believe it." Then the preacher quoted

Romans 10:9-10. "Don't you want to take this Saviour as your Saviour, Tod—One that sticketh closer
than a brother—One Who would go even unto the end,
and not like the old gang that leaves and forsakes?"

That morning Tod Sloane confessed Jesus Christ as
his personal Saviour, and there was joy in the presence
of the angels.

It was only a few weeks later that Tod Sloane began to ride for the King of kings and Lord of lords.
Said this pastor, "I was with him once or twice a day
after that, and also on the last day of his life—just
an hour and a half before he went home. The last
words he said to me were these: "I am riding my last
race; it won't be long before I will be standing in front
of the Judge's stand, weighing in."

"Yes, Tod," I said, "you are riding a winning race
and when you stand with saddle and whip in hand,
ready to be weighed in, you will tip the scales and
the Great Judge will not disqualify you."

"We prayed together," continued the preacher, "and
then I said 'good-bye,' but before leaving him for the
last time I asked him: 'Do you really know Him as
your personal Saviour?' 'Yes, sir,' answered Tod
Sloane, 'and He is precious to me.' "

Who is a Christian? This—one who believes on the
Lord Jesus Christ. Respectability does not save, religiousness does not save, good works cannot save; but,
praise be to God, simple faith can. "To him that worketh not, but believeth"—this is the Word of God. Our
faith is accounted for righteousness. May God help
every one of you to have this faith.

II.

THE CONVERSION OF SAUL OF TARSUS
Acts IX.
THE STUDY

The Occasion.

OUR STORY opens with the first persecution of the Church. We noted in Chapter eight that the Church leaders had been scattered abroad, but now the Jewish leaders were endeavoring to break up every local assembly, and to destroy the name and the faith of Jesus from Jerusalem and from the surrounding territory. Stephen had been stoned to death, while a young man by the name of Saul held the clothes of those who did the stoning. Saul now comes on the scene, breathing out threatenings and slaughter against the people of God, and is on his way to Damascus to destroy the little church of faithful in that place, when the occurrences of the story take place.

The Subject.

Saul of Tarsus is too well known for any need of a survey of his life to be made here. We may just note, however, that, at the time of his conversion he is one of the most promising young Pharisees in Jerusalem. Undoubtedly, he would have made a name for himself among his people. We must note also that

according to world standards, he was a most unlikely
subject for conversion to Christianity. His hard-headed-
ness, his bitterness against the faith, his tendency to
ignore truth in that direction, made him such a person.

The Agent.

Here the student must note the uniqueness of the
situation. There are no human agents operative. The
risen and glorified Christ is here the personal worker.
Paul was the ascended Christ's own and only convert,
and stands unique in the history of conversion. The
significance of this experience of Saul is both individual and prophetic. At a later day, he declares himself to be a Jew born out of due time. Undoubtedly,
the manner of his conversion was both Jewish and Christian; Jewish in that the Lord Jesus appeared to him
personally, as He will appear one day to a remnant
of Israel during the Tribulation, and Christian, in that
he became a member of the Body of Christ, being baptized in the Spirit into that Body at his conversion.

The Accompaniments.

These, too, are unique, and without parallel in history. Furthermore, we have no right to expect an exact
duplication of them, or of the situation in which they appear, in any conversion to-day. The supernatural,
bright, vivid and unmistakable, predominates here. The
student will find very little help for modern religious
experience in the accompaniments of Saul's conversion,
but he will find much to strengthen his faith in the

miraculous intervention of God, through Jesus Christ, in the life of this man.

The Results.

The immediate results are very startling. We find an instantaneously changed man, with a changed purpose. The far-reaching results are comprehended only by a careful study of the life and ministry of the Apostle Paul, a man who all but brought the Roman Empire to his feet through the power of his preaching of the Gospel of the Lord Jesus Christ.

Significant Lessons.

A warning should be given zealous folks expecting to reproduce such phenomena in present-day conversions. It is highly improbable and decidedly unnecessary. However, encouragement may be taught through a manifestation of the fact that no case is too great for God. Prevailing prayer looses a power which may bring modern Sauls to their knees, in repentance. This man is the type of those for whom little else avails. Some have claimed Saul to be the convert of the dying Stephen, but there is no warrant for such an assumption, for after the death of Stephen, Saul was more vicious than ever in his persecuting of the Church. No; Saul is Christ's own and only convert, but undoubtedly great prayer had been made for him, and great results followed.

THE SERMON

THE SALVATION OF A SINCERE MAN—DEAD WRONG

Acts IX.

THE NINTH chapter of the Acts records the most remarkable conversion in all history, not only for the experience itself, but for its results to the world. Saul's experience is absolutely unique; there never was another experience like his, and there will not be another in this dispensation. I remember years ago hearing Billy Sunday, preaching on the Apostle Paul, tell the story of the man who came to the evangelist, saying he was a believer, in a sense, and he expected to be saved one day, but he said he wanted an experience like Paul's; he was waiting for Jesus Christ to appear to him in person. I shall never forget the sarcasm with which Sunday told of his reply to this man. "Why," said the evangelist, "what right have you to expect that Jesus will do for you what He did for the Apostle Paul? Why, man alive, Paul was big game, and God could afford to do an unusual thing to get him; but you can't expect God to use a Gatling gun to get a canary like you!"

Saul, as his name was before his conversion, was the ascended Christ's own and only convert. Practically every one else has been converted by hearing some one tell the story of Jesus and believing that story; but Saul was different. His conversion is typically Jewish—as a remnant of Israel will be saved at a later time. You remember how the Prophet has de-

clared that the time will come when a remnant of Jews
in the land of Palestine under persecution will flee to
the desert and there meet their Messiah face to face,
and they shall say, "What are these wounds in Thy
hands?" and he will reply, "These are they which I
received in the house of my friends." And then they
shall weep and mourn in His presence. Paul himself
declared that he was a Jew born out of due time, or
of premature birth. By that, undoubtedly, he meant that
his type of conversion was that which the Jews will
experience in the Tribulation period, when the Lord
appears to them in person as He did to Saul on the
Damascus road.

The conversion of Saul was remarkable and mo-
mentous. No journey was ever taken by man, save
the journey up Calvary's hill on the part of the Son
of God, which meant so much to the race and its redemption as did Saul's journey to Damascus. The conversion of Saul of Tarsus is the next great event after
the Resurrection and Pentecost. It takes place in
the New Testament in the same significant way that the
call of Abraham does in the Old Testament. It is the
beginning of a world-wide outreach of the Gospel—
God's first stroke in bringing the Gospel to our fore-
bears, whether they be Anglo-Saxons, Franks, Gauls, or
Norsemen—and finally to our own lives. Surely, then,
this life experience is worthy of our careful study, and
should yield a wealth of lessons!

It is an experience directly opposite to that which
we studied in the preceding chapter. There were very

few unusual accompaniments of the conversion of the
Ethiopian Eunuch, and what is more, he was a seeker
after truth. Saul was a persecutor of those who believed
the truth. God works in diversified ways and under
many conditions. We shall note primarily the intense
sincerity of Saul, and at the same time note that he
was blasphemously wrong in his attitude toward Christianity.

Now, *sincerity is an admirable virtue,* "Sincerity
is the face of the soul." Carlyle declared: "Sincerity
is the first characteristic of all men in any way heroic."
Shakespeare wrote: "To thine own self be true, and
it must follow, as the night to the day, thou canst not
then be false to any man."

But a place can be given to sincerity which it has
no right to occupy, for sincerity misdirected is a very
dangerous thing. This terrible misappropriation finds
its chief expression in the realm of religion, where multitudes are sincere and sincerely wrong.

Earnestness is no guarantee of truth, as passiveness
is no guarantee of error. Earnestness and error are most
destructive forces, while earnestness and truth are all
but unconquerable. We have both conditions illustrated
in the law, blameless."

I. Paul Was Sincere But Wrong in His Belief.

Paul (as he was known after his conversion) was
brought up in a strict Jewish home in Tarsus of Cilicia,
a Grecian town of culture, where Grecian debauchery
had taken toll of many lives, but Paul's strict training
reacted against it. In Philippians, third chapter, he de-

clares with great pride: "If any other man thinketh that he hath whereof he might trust in the flesh, I more. Circumcised the eighth day, of the stock of Israel, of the tribe of Benjamin, an Hebrew of the Hebrews, as touching the law a Pharisee. Concerning zeal, persecuting the church, touching the righteousness which is in the law, blameless."

All this means that he was a strict Judaist. He was a non-believer in Christ; he regarded Him as a fake, an imposter who had suffered a just death upon a cross. Christ's disciples were lunatics to him, deluded fanatics, better off dead than living, and though deadly sincere in those things, he was, at the same time, dead wrong.

Now, you may have no religion and be sincere about it; you may live up to the light you imagine you have, but you're wrong and God says to you, get right. You may have a religion and be sincere in practicing it, but if it is not God's revealed religion, your sincerity is but carrying you that much faster to perdition.

Adherents to false faith are almost invariably intensely sincere. The Mohammedan, for example, kneels and prays three times a day, with his face toward Mecca, but does not know God, or Christ, or salvation. The Buddhist brings his sacrifice to the temple in all sincerity; he submits himself to bodily tortures such as sitting in a circle of fire, lying on a bed of spikes, holding up an arm until the muscles shrivel and die; but he is no nearer God. With all these efforts, sin-

cere though he may be, he is only farther and farther
away from truth. The African mother who throws her
baby to the crocodile in the Nile, or the Indian mother
who sacrifices her baby, may be sincere, but nevertheless both mothers are sinful. So with you. Your sincerity will not save you; you must be right with God,
or else you will hear the words: "Depart from me, ye
cursed, I never knew you."

Some time ago a man bought a ticket in New York
for the city of Chicago, but he got on the wrong train,
and when the conductor came around to take the ticket,
noticing the man was on the wrong train, he insisted
that the man get off at the next stop; but the man re-
monstrated and said: "Listen, here, conductor, I
bought this ticket in all sincerity, I want to go to Chicago, I bought a ticket for Chicago, and I was sincere
in buying the ticket, and I paid sincere money for the
ticket, and I was sincere when I got on this train. I
can't see any reason why I shouldn't land in Chicago.
Why should I get off this train when I boarded it in
all sincerity?" "You're a fool, no matter how sincere
you are," replied the conductor. "You'll never reach
Chicago on this train; it's going in another direction."
So with you. No matter how sincere you may be, unless
you're on board the Gospel train, through faith in
Jesus Christ you'll never arrive in the Land of God's
Eternal Day.

II. NOTE NOW THAT PAUL WAS SINCERE BUT
WRONG IN HIS ACTIVITIES.

The first picture we have of Saul, is his connection with the death of the martyr Stephen. He steps on the stage of sacred history, guarding the clothes of those who threw the stones, and the record tells us that "Saul was consenting unto his death."

But though he comes to us in this dramatic role, Saul was not a hoodlum, but was a sincere religionist who believed that Stephen ought to die for violating the first commandment, which reads: "Thou shalt have no other gods before me." Stephen worshipped Jesus Christ as God, and Saul deemed him, thereby, to be an idolator worthy of death.

Undoubtedly, he was so stirred by what he thought were blasphemies of this sort from the sect of Christians that he felt called of God to stamp it out mercilessly and completely, and seems to have set about doing the job single-handed. In Acts 8: 3, we read: "As for Saul, he made havoc of the church, entering into every house and hailing men and women, committed them to prison."

I'll guarantee that Saul got up every morning, prayed fervently for help in this matter, and every evening devoutly thanked God for what he had been able to accomplish. You will remember that Jesus forewarned His followers of this sort of spirit, when He told that the time would come that they who killed them, would think that "they were doing God a favor." Saul was such an one as this. He was wrong, though sincere—dead wrong.

And you may feel that this world would be better off without what you call superstitious Christians;

you may think that your good works will save you.
But you are wrong. Saul was a fine character, had
a warm heart, and a fervent spirit. He meant well,
but he did wrong.

III. PAUL WAS SINCERE AND RIGHT AFTER HIS CONVERSION.

Here is where the drama of the story comes in. Saul
had heard that, in Damascus of Syria, where God had
been so merciful to Naaman, the leper, was one of the
places where the fugitives had taken refuge, and that
they were busily at work, making converts. So, "breathing out threatenings and slaughter," Saul started on
his way to that city with letters giving him permission
to capture and extradite those folks, carry them captives to Jerusalem, probably to their death. It was a
long journey to Damascus. Saul was nearing his des-
tination, when a light brighter than the noonday Syrian
sun dimmed Paul's sight and felled him to the ground,
and set him to crying and groveling in the dust.

Then a voice was heard saying: "Saul, Saul, why
persecutest thou me?" How remarkable, that God knew
Saul's name! Ah, yes, God knows your name; you're
not hid from Him and He'll seek you and speak to your
heart. He knows you through and through; thought and
imagination; word and deed; joint and marrow.

Saul must have been astounded at the question,
"Why persecutest thou me?" He could have replied:
"Why, I never saw you, I never persecuted you, I never
spoke a word against you. These men and women that I
am hailing into prison are not you!" But therein Saul

had made his great mistake. These men and women he had hailed to prison were members of the Body of Christ, and Jesus was truly saying to him: "Saul, the brutal stones you piled upon Stephen, cutting his flesh, hurt Me; whenever you put one of My people in prison you put Me in prison."

One of the beauties of the relationship of Christ and His Church is that our Lord never considers Himself separate from His people. They are crucified together with Him, they are buried together and risen together, they live together with Him, they are made to sit together in heavenly places in Christ Jesus, and they will meet together with Him in the air and so be for ever with Him.

Oh, I know what some folks are saying: "I'll not go forward, I'll not allow the preacher to convince me, I'll not join the Church and get in with those self-righteous people. I know them!"

Listen: Jesus says: "You're not rejecting them, you are rejecting Me. Why persecutest thou me? Your relationship is to the Son of God. You can't separate Christ from His people. There is a philosophy to-day which attempts to do so, but, however unworthy we may be, our great Christ says: "Strike them and you strike Me; reject them and you reject Me."

And Saul, subdued, blind and beaten, says: "Who art Thou, Lord?" He apparently recognized the commanding character of the voice though he did not know who spoke. Then the astounding reply comes back: "I am Jesus whom thou persecutest." Imagine Saul's surprise—horror, for that matter! To Saul, Jesus was a dead man, disgraced and hated. Did not the Pharisees and the Roman soldiers exult over the fact that they had put Him out of the way? To Saul, Jesus was a dead blasphemer, buried and disreputable of memory. Yet here, in an aura of bright light never before seen on land or sea, stands One who says, "I am Jesus whom thou persecutest!"

Oh, don't you know that Christ lives? You may think of Him as a dead Christ, you may use his name in blasphemy; but when you use the name of Jesus, you're using the name of a living Person.

What a tumult must have raged in Saul's soul! You know the hardest three words to say in the English language—in any language, for that matter—are: "I am wrong." The mind is very reluctant to admit the failure and error of its conclusions; the heart rebels against higher authority. Poor Saul! *His journey was ended,* and his life's ambitions came tumbling about him as a house of cards.

As though seeing, perhaps, the turmoil of his soul, Jesus then says—doubtless very tenderly—to His stricken quarry: "It is hard for thee to kick against the pricks." The figure is an Oriental one, as you well know. The ox driver wields a long pole, at the end of which is fixed a sharpened iron with which he prods the animal. If fractious and rebellious, the beast will kick against the goad, injuring and infuriating itself by the wounds it receives; but, if patient, it will heed the prodding of the goad and go on its way. Jesus was instructing Saul when He said: "It is hard for

thee to kick against the pricks." I wonder if you are
kicking against the goad—if a voice is whispering to
your soul that you are not merely fighting a creed or
cult, but Jesus? If your heart is reluctant to admit it, as
mine was, long ago, I beg of you, do not kick against
the goad!

An old salt once said to a young seaman: "Aboard
a man o' war, son, there's just one choice—duty, or
mutiny." And in this matter of the Gospel, there is
just one choice—rejection or acceptance. Your conscience tells you of sin needing forgiveness, of a soul
needing cleansing; the Spirit tells you of your need
of surrender, and your whole nature cries out in rebel-
lion; but don't, for your sake—for God's sake—kick
against the goad!

As for Saul, it was all settled with him right there.
He was conquered. "What wilt thou have me to do?"
is his first question as a Christian. What a change!
See him as he enters Damascus, no longer a proud
Pharisee, riding majestically with the pomp and au-
thority of an inquisitor, but a stricken man trembling,
groping, clinging to the hand of his guide, in darkness—
Christ-conquered!

We read, further in the story, of his visit to Ananias
and of the tenderness shown him by this brother in
Christ; of the restoration of his sight, of his baptism
and infilling with the Holy Spirit, and his going forth
on his great ministry. The story is too well known to
need retelling in detail, but we want to note Saul's attitude. We thank God for one thing, that is,—*he never
looked back*. The record of his life from that day

forward seems to have been one of continuous obedience. "What wilt Thou have me to do?" seems to
be the norm of his Christian experience.

And if you are willing to ask, "What wilt Thou
have me to do?" God's answer will be: "This is the
will of God, that you believe on Him whom He has
sent." And again, "If thou shalt confess with thy
mouth the Lord Jesus and believe in thine heart that
God hath raised Him from the dead, thou shalt be
saved."

Some years ago, a British chaplain, talking to a Boys'
Brigade unit, told the story of Wellington's victories in
the Peninsular War. After one of the battles the defeated French officers repaired to Wellington's tent and,
with characteristic French extravagance, declared to the
British commander that they were not ashamed to be
beaten by the greatest general in Europe, and continued
with a great deal of flowery praise. Wellington heard
them sternly and coldly. When they had finished their
profuse statements he simply said: "Gentlemen, your
swords!" Instantly, the Frenchmen yielded their swords
in token of surrender; then, Wellington could be, and
was, gracious to his captives. "Now, young men," con-
cluded the chaplain, "Jesus wants your swords, that is,
your yielded hearts."

In like manner, may I repeat that Jesus wants your
yielded hearts? You may be sincere, you may be earnest, you may think you're right, like Saul of Tarsus,
but until you know God through the Lord Jesus as your
personal Saviour, in spite of all your sincerity, you
are wrong, dead wrong. May God help you to get right.

III.

THE CONVERSION OF CORNELIUS

Acts 10.

THE STUDY

The Occasion.

HERE IS a long and fascinating story which should be read and studied with care. There is a subtle intermingling of the natural and supernatural which we believe normally accompanies conversion. The supernatural is not as clearly seen and comprehended, to-day, as in those days of "open vision"; but for those who have eyes to see, it is present in all true conversion. As in Chapter eight, we have here a prepared subject and agent, but in entirely different ways.

The Subject.

Cornelius was a Roman centurion stationed at Caesarea, in Palestine, and reputed to have been of a distinguished Roman family. He was probably a Jewish proselyte, but not a full proselyte. There is a real distinction between the two. Full proselytes of Judaism were such as submitted themselves entirely to the rites and ordinances of the Jews, were circumcised, and thereby entered into all the privileges of the covenant people. It is apparent that Cornelius was not one of

45

these. It has been suggested that he was a "proselyte of the gate." Of course, in the thinking and attitude of the Jews, such an one was still a Gentile and vastly inferior. It is evident that he was a religious man, devout, fearing God, giving much alms, and praying to God always. His faith in God is manifested supremely in his prayer-life. When a man prays, he certainly has some faith in God.

The Agent.

The Apostle Peter is God's instrument here. He is making the second use of the keys of the Kingdom, the first use of which he made on the day of Pentecost, opening up the Gospel to the Jews. Now, in the household of Cornelius, he is bringing the Gospel to the Gentiles. God's preparation of Peter should be studied with care. The removal of Jewish bigotry by means of the vision of the unclean things and the statement, "What God has cleansed that call not thou common." Peter's method of approach to Cornelius and the other Gentiles is also worthy of careful study.

The Accompaniments.

The supernatural predominates to the close of the transaction. There are visions, tongues, and other divine demonstrations. In the midst of all the outward manifestations, however, the student must note the normal procedure in conversion. The Word is preached, believed, and the Spirit's regenerating power comes in answer to faith.

Results.

The immediate results are the conversion of Cornelius and his household. The far-reaching results include the opening of the door of the Gospel to the Gentiles. Peter doubtless thought that this turning aside to the Gentiles was a mere innovation, an interlude on the part of God. Little did he realize that this door was to swing wide to the great Gentile nations, and that, eventually, the Gentiles would make up the major portion of the Body of the Lord Jesus Christ, while the Jews would turn aside from the Gospel in unbelief.

Significant Lessons.

Racial differences should never be a deterrent to personal soul winning, and there should be no adaptation of the Gospel to please the worldly prominent. The gist of Peter's message is the same as that which he preached on the day of Pentecost to the Jews. Note, however, that there is no condemnation of the Gentiles. The Jews are held accountable for the crucifixion of Jesus; the Gentiles are accountable only for rejecting His mercy. Here is a type of the power used in winning big men. Note, however, that human shrewdness was not used by Peter, but the wisdom of God in the Gospel. The choosing of key-men is God's prerogative, not ours. Preaching the Gospel to them is our privilege.

THE SERMON
CAN A RELIGIOUS MAN BE SAVED?
Acts 10.

IF IN all the world, there can be found a single man who does not need Jesus Christ and His Gospel, then Christianity collapses. This is a startling statement,

and yet I challenge any who have long desired to put
Christianity out of business to bring one man who is
without sin—one man who does not need salvation.
The presence of that man will disprove the fundamental claims of Christianity and put it out of existence; and every honest preacher will have to quit his
job and seek some other way of earning a living!

You may ask—why is that? My reply is that *Christianity presupposes a lost world*. It declares boldly
that "all we like sheep have gone astray; we have
turned every one to his own way, and the Lord has
laid upon him the iniquity of us all." Jesus declared
He came to "seek and to save that which was lost."
Paul says, "All have sinned and come short of the
glory of God," and "there is none righteous, no, not
one." John says, "If we say we have no sin, we deceive
ourselves, and, if we say that we have not sinned, we
make God a liar."

Now this is a hard pill for the world to swallow,
because of its pride and self-sufficiency, because of the
boast of human achievement, and the evolutionary philosophy that claims man is slowly but surely advancing
to perfection, and that he needs not so much a Saviour
as someone to give him a start along the pathway of his
progress.

We are brought face to face in this study with the
doctrine of total depravity. This is the doctrine of
which little has been heard in the preachments of the
Church in recent years. But the condition of men's
hearts which calls forth a statement of the doctrine has

not changed. The fact of the matter is, that condition has been intensified with the passing of the years.

By the doctrine of total depravity, we mean that the sinner is totally destitute of that love to God which constitutes the fundamental and all-inclusive demand of the law; that all of his tendencies and dispositions are toward sin and not toward righteousness. The sinner is possessed of an aversion to God which, though not always apparent, nevertheless is in God's sight active enmity, and it is manifest at least as soon as God's will comes into conflict with his own. Every spiritually minded student of human nature knows that sinful man has a corrupted faculty and does not evolve toward perfection, but rather has constant progress in depravity, and he has no recuperative powers of his own, but waits for the power of God in regeneration to change his nature.

It is a part of the belligerent apostasy of our day to deny and scoff at this doctrine of human depravity. The late Dr. W. H. P. Faunce, former President of Brown University, made this statement: "Those who believe in total depravity must be unfortunate in their friends." And his statement manifests a tendency in the Church to-day. Preachers are giving their people "sugar and spice and everything nice"; our theology, to-day, has become, as some one has said, a "lavender-water" theology, and there is no blood in it nor any power, nor any condemnation of sin. Now let us not make a mistake; by total depravity, we do not mean that men are as bad as they can be, nor that they have done, in their natural condition, all that they could do for evil. Most men possess certain amiable qualities; many unsaved men have high virtues according to human standards. By total depravity we mean that a sinful condition affects *the whole man*—intellect, feeling, heart, and will, and that, until the love of God comes into his heart by regeneration, he is destitute of that love, and has no ability to do anything to please God. A watch does not need to have every wheel and part of its mechanism destroyed in order to be rendered useless; it is totally useless when its main spring is broken—when it fails to tell time; in other words, when it fails to function in the realm and for the purpose for which it was created. *This is man's condition under sin.*

The Gospel is a startling thing; it makes people less religious and more righteous. The depraved man is ofttimes very religious, but his religion is an abomination to God. The Gospel makes him righteous, with the righteousness of Jesus Christ imputed and imparted unto him.

Now here's Cornelius, who apparently did not need the Gospel. The Scriptures declare that he was "a devout man and one that feared God with all his house, which gave much alms to the people and prayed to God alway." That's a testimony worthy of consideration. I declare to you that eighty per cent of the churches to-day would have received him just as he was; but God would not receive him as he was. Why? He was a religious man; why was he not all right?

I. Some Remarkable Characteristics of
the Man.

He was a devout man. That means a religious man. It is profitable to study the centurions of the Bible. Every one of them was a man of high character, and we are told that this man was not only of noble character but of noble lineage. Dr. Campbell Morgan says of him: "We know certainly that Cornelius was a Roman soldier. He may have been a patrician or a plebeian. There was a great Roman family of the Cornealian patricians and there was also a great family of enfranchised slaves, Cornelii; for an emperor had enfranchised a number of slaves and had given them his own name. This man may have been of one or the other family; which, we can not tell. But unmistakably he was devoutly religious and he was no mere religious dabbler. He was earnest in the matter. It is apparent that he sought escape from the idolatry of the Romans of his day. He saw the emptiness of paganism, and sought a knowledge of the true God. This is commendable."

This spirit is not absent to-day. Men are indeed seeking reality. One of the reasons why the Church is coming into disrepute with so many is because it has turned aside from reality to men's ethereal philosophy and has dealt much with human vagaries and empty sentiment rather than getting down to the hard facts of existence and presenting a Gospel that is the salvation of men's souls and the alleviation of the hardships of existence through refuge in God. Oh, that the Church would give reality to men! We should have a glorious revival.

He was a God-fearing man, that is to say, he was reverent. He reverenced God. There were quite a number of Gentile "God-fearers" during New Testament times. These men and women followed Jewish ethics; they prayed to Jehovah and gave alms; many of them were called friends of the Jewish synagogues because they helped support the religious life of their Gentile communities through the synagogues which were established in the cities and towns.

It is not surprising that this should be so. Intelligent folks know that there is a God. Atheism is a fool's faith, and you don't find intelligent people turning to atheism in large numbers. They may not be Christians, they may not have given themselves to Jesus Christ, but they do not deny the existence of God and the possibilities of human responsibility to Him.

We note also that *he was benevolent and charitable.* This shows an admirable attitude toward his fellow men. Many unsaved people are very charitable. Human goodness is a fact with which we have to deal. Unfortunately, some unsaved people seem to be more generous along this line than some who know the Gospel. We might truthfully say that two great hindrances to the on-going of the Gospel are uncharitable Christians and charitable sinners. Philanthropy apart from Christ is deadly in more ways than one.

We note, also, that *he was a praying man,* and he was not a mere pagan prayer apparently. He didn't enter into the superstition of beads and prayer-wheels and prayer-rugs of the Mohammedans. He was a successful prayer; he prayed down an angel. A good many of God's children have never prayed anything down, to their knowledge. Cornelius' earnestness moved the heart and the hand of God, and so successful was his praying that there was angelic interference in his behalf.

We ask again, what more could this man need? Surely Christianity fails here. Here's a man who needs not the message of the Gospel, for he has everything necessary without it.

II. GOD'S APPRECIATION OF THIS MAN'S REMARKABLE QUALITIES.

As we have noted, God sends an angel messenger to instruct Cornelius. We believe this was because he was thoroughly honest. Cornelius sought God, but God sought Cornelius. God never yet ignored an honest seeker.

We learn that his prayers and alms are recorded. It seems to me that we have here an answer to one of the great problems of prayer. The question is often asked, are the prayers of the unsaved answered? And we can reply that they are heard but cannot be fully answered, because in this dispensation they are not acceptable without the finished work of Jesus Christ operative in the life of the one who prays. The one who comes to God in the age of grace must be a redeemed soul under the blood of Jesus Christ, and he must recognize the high-priestly work of the Lord Jesus as his intercessor before the throne of grace, so that the limitations to the prayers of Cornelius were that, *though God heard his prayers, they were unacceptable; and, though his alms were recorded, they were insufficient.* Something more needed to be done. You will note that the record says that these things came up before God as a memorial, or, as Moffatt puts it, "a sacrifice to be remembered."

It would appear that God keeps a note book. God is willing to move heaven and earth for an earnest man's salvation. That's just exactly what He did do. He moved heaven and sent an angel to Cornelius, and He moved earth and prepared the narrow and bigoted Peter to be the preacher of the Gospel to this consecrated Gentile. Yet for all his excellent qualities and for all of God's appreciation of his remarkable characteristics, this man needed to be saved. He was a good man, but he was not a saved man, and there's a definite difference.

The story is told of two men who started out to hear a concert, which both were desirous of enjoying. It seems that they were both hard pressed financially; one had a dollar, the other had fifty cents; but, when they got to the concert hall, they made the discovery that the tickets were two dollars for the cheapest seats. On the way to the concert hall, the man with the dollar had good naturedly chided the fellow with but fifty cents and said: "There is no chance for you getting in, I don't believe there's a seat as cheap as fifty cents in the house, although I'm sure that I can get one for a dollar. You will be shut out while I will be let in!" When the discovery was made that the cheapest seat was two dollars, the fellow with the fifty cents had a great laugh at the fellow with the dollar. "Say, brother," he said, "you've been boasting all the while that you are twice as rich as I, but it makes little difference as regards this concert—you, with a dollar, didn't get any nearer the show than I did with fifty cents!"

This is a picture of man's morality. Undoubtedly, some men are better than others, but none are good enough to meet God's standard, which is absolute holiness. Therefore, all men are rejected. As Romans tells us: "All are reckoned under sin that God might be merciful to all." Now I know that some students of this passage will remind me that in the verses 34, 35 of our study-chapter, Peter says: "Of a truth I perceive that God is no respecter of persons: But in every nation he that feareth him, and worketh righteousness, is accepted with him." But I am sure that a further study of the Word of God will show that that term "accepted" has definite limitations to it. One may be accepted for certain things, such as accepted as a candidate for salvation, but certainly not accepted as a saved person. All men are the objects of God's grace; all men are acceptable unto God through the death of Jesus Christ, but all men need to be saved through faith in the Saviour.

III. God's Method of Saving a Religious Man.

There is before us a whole series of events which shows God's interest in man and the divine plan and program for individual salvation.

First of all, note that the angel visitor said to Cornelius: "Send men to Joppa, and call for one Simon, whose surname is Peter." A remarkable order that, when you thing of it. Why didn't the angel tell the story of salvation to Cornelius? Well, he was not permitted, and doubtless he was not able. God's instruments for the preaching of the Gospel are only those who have experienced the saving power of the Gospel. Oh, the privilege of it! And to think that we take such little advantage of our high and holy privilege. The late S. D. Gordon, in his quiet way, used to tell the imaginative story of Jesus going back to heaven after His death and resurrection. When met at the pearly gates, He was asked by one of the heavenly hosts what He had done. He told the story of the out-working of salvation through His death and resurrection and of the leaving of just a few individuals behind to tell the story to a lost world; and then a heavenly being in anxious tones asked: "But supposing these men fail? Supposing they don't tell the story?" Quietly, the Lord Jesus says: "If they fail, I fail, I have no other plan."

Peter himself has a vision, as we have already noted, that takes away the natural prejudice of the Jew against the Gentile, and he goes on his way to Caesarea. There he finds Cornelius waiting for him with his whole household gathered together and near friends added, so that they, too, could hear the Gospel. Peter begins his message with a very humble declaration, for a Jew speaking to a Gentile, by declaring that he has discovered that God is no respecter of persons; or, to give a literal translation, that God is no

"respecter of a face." When one considers the essential
difference between the face of a Jew and the face of a
Gentile, you will see that this is a significant statement.
It would seem that the Jew had the idea that God loved
only a Jewish face and cared nothing for a Gentile one.

But Peter recognizes the fact that the Gospel was
to the Jew first, for he declares that his message is,
"the word which God sent unto the children of Israel,
preaching peace by Jesus Christ," and that this word
had been published throughout all Judea, beginning at
Galilee, after the baptism which John preached. He
continues on telling of the good works and miracles
of the Lord Jesus, and then emphasizes the fact that
He was crucified, that they slew Him and hanged Him
on a tree.

Peter not only preached the Cross, but he preached
the resurrection. He told them that God had raised up
Jesus the third day and showed Him openly. He declared also for his own commission to preach the
Gospel, and like every true preacher of the Word he
made an application, declaring: "To him give all the
prophets witness, that through his name whosoever believeth in him shall receive remission of sins." To Peter
unlike many in our day, the sermon was not an end—
it was a means to an end. Peter preached with purpose; not to entertain, but to bring men to a saving
knowledge of God in Christ. The preacher had no opportunity to finish his message before God began to do
a work. It's quite apparent that Cornelius and his household believed the Gospel and immediately the Holy
Spirit fell on all them which heard the Word. Peter

was hardly prepared for this and we are told that he
was astonished to discover that God was willing to pour
out His Holy Spirit upon the Gentiles. The believers
baptized in the Holy Spirit were then baptized in water,
and the initial work of the Gospel was done in their
lives.

Peter, later, rehearsing the whole matter before the
council in Jerusalem, tells how the angel had told
Cornelius to send to Joppa and call Simon, whose surname is Peter, who shall tell thee *Words* whereby thou
and all thy house shall be saved. He shall tell thee
Words! What a blessed truth! The Gospel is a matter of
words and belief of words. Even as Jesus said: "Verily,
verily, I say unto you, he that heareth *my word* and
believeth on him that sent me hath everlasting life and
shall not come into condemnation, but is passed from
death unto life."

This experience is what every religious man needs.
To hear the Gospel of the Crucified and Risen Christ,
and to accept it for the forgiveness of sins and for
the gift of the Holy Spirit. Oh, the deluded millions
in our day, who think that they can be saved by good
works! Oh, the multitude that surely must hear on
that awful day from the lips of the Lord Jesus (who
to-day would save them if they would but come) the
words—"Depart from Me, I never knew you." Oh,
that some earnest but mistaken and deluded soul might
hear this message to-night and might be shaken out of
his lethargy, and might cry out unto God for salvation.

A number of years ago, on New Year's Day, I was
sitting by my radio, on a cold, snowy afternoon, lis-

tening to the broadcast of a football game emanating
from the Rose Bowl in sunny California. The teams,
as I recall, were Georgia Tech. and the University of
Southern California. It was an exciting game and I
listened to the cheers and the words of the announcer.
Suddenly, something unusual happened. The cheering
of the crowd stopped and there was a deadly hush;
the announcer choked and stumbled and stammered and
tried to tell what he saw, but he was so excited that
words did not seem sufficient to describe what was
going on. We later learned what took place. It seems
that a young and active player who had recently been
elected to the captaincy of the Southern California team,
and who had been playing a fine game hitherto, had
got the ball, and in the wild scramble he had been
hit hard and turned around; but he wasn't down, and
when he recovered his senses sufficiently he began to
run. The crowd began to cheer, and then they saw
what had taken place, and the cheer ended in a groan,
and then there was an awful silence. The young man
ran on with enthusiasm; only to be pulled down by
one of his own men, after he had made a sixty-five
yard run in *the wrong direction!* When he got to his
feet, not knowing who had pulled him down, he asked,
"Why doesn't the crowd cheer?" And in the excitement
one of his teammates said: "You fool, you have lost
us the game. You ran in the wrong direction." It is
said that the young man staggered and wept, so
stricken was he because of his mistake. Now that young
man ran as enthusiastically as though he were running
in the right direction; he thought he *was* running in

the right direction, but he had been hit and turned
around.

And I thought, as I pondered the story, what a picture it was of many souls running the race of life,
hoping for salvation at the end of the way, thinking
that their good lives, their prayers, their alms, their
religiousness will win them favor with God, when the
Word solemnly says, "Except a man be born again, he
cannot see the kingdom of God."

Oh, friends, the devil and all the forces of evil
will cheer you while you run in the wrong direction,
but I'm trying to halt you and tell you that the faster
you travel, the farther you'll land away from God; but
if you'll only turn and by God's grace head in the
right direction through faith in Jesus Christ, then all
heaven will applaud one day when you stand faultless
in His presence.

> *Turn thee, O lost one, careworn and weary,*
> *Lo! the Good Shepherd is pleading to-day;*
> *Seeking to save thee, waiting to cleanse thee:*
> *Haste to receive Him—no longer delay!*
>
> *List to His message, think of His mercy!*
> *Sinless, yet bearing thy sins on the tree;*
> *Perfect remission, life everlasting,*
> *Through His atonement He offers to thee.*
>
> *Come in the old way, come in the true way,*
> *Enter through Jesus, for He is the Door;*
> *He is the Shepherd, tenderly calling:*
> *Come in thy weakness and wander no more.*

IV.

THE CONVERSION OF SERGIUS PAULUS

Acts 13.

THE STUDY

The Occasion.

IN THE event before us, the Church is sending out her first missionaries. It is therefore an auspicious occasion. Also, Paul is beginning his first missionary journey, and there are far-reaching effects. The devout little church at Antioch in Syria gets a world vision under the leadership of the Spirit of God, and becomes the mother church of Gentile Christendom. The members had ministered unto the Lord and fasted and prayed, and the Holy Ghost had said, "Separate me Barnabas and Saul for the work whereunto I have called them," and in due time the Holy Ghost sent them forth on their great missionary enterprise. They had gone to Salamis and had passed through the isle unto Paphos, and there they came into conflict with the devil and his emissaries. The situation resolved itself into a contest over the soul of a man. Here we see the drama that has been reenacted a million times.

The Subject.

Sergius Paulus was undoubtedly a Roman and a representative of the Roman government. He would therefore normally be a materialist, and usually men of his type were hard-hearted individuals. Whether he had any knowledge of the Gospel previous to the coming of Paul and Barnabas we do not know. But it is evident that he was a man inquiring after the truth. Whatever may have been the human factors entering into this, undoubtedly the Holy Spirit had done a preparatory work in the man's heart. He must have been a man of unusual intelligence for he is reported to have been the ruler of the Isle of Cyprus. He is called a deputy in the Authorized Version and a proconsul in the Revised Version. Whatever previous knowledge of the truth he may have received, it is certain that he had received a great deal of false teaching from Elymas, the sorcerer.

The Agents.

The agents of this conversion, generally, are Paul and Silas, but Paul primarily, and the Holy Ghost finally, for it is apparent that the contest is between the Holy Spirit and the devil himself.

The Accompaniments.

Here is a conflict, tense and bitter. The first recorded battle of false faith against the true in the apostolic era. We see, also, these important factors: first, the *interposition of spiritual force;* second, an *adverse miracle.* There are few of these in the New Testament; Jesus performed but two which are recorded in all of the Gospels. Elymas is stricken blind for a season. Third, there is astonishment because of the miracle, and faith results. The belief in this case comes more, it would seem, from the miracle than from the preaching. As is ofttimes the case in outstanding conversions, there are startling contrasts here. Light for Paulus; darkness for Elymas. The central scene of the drama is satanic opposition. This opposition comes through a typical *child of the devil who is an apostate, a teacher of false faith.*

The Results.

We have already partially noted these. Apart from the salvation of Sergius Paulus, it is important to note that the devil is openly and dramatically defeated. The mission upon which Paul and Barnabas are launched triumphs over Satan's opposition, even as Jesus triumphed at the beginning of His ministry. Defeat here for the apostles would mean a wrecked voyage for the Gospel.

Significant Lessons.

Learn some valuable lessons from the devil. He keeps his eye on the working of God's children, especially when they are directed by the Holy Ghost. He always resists beginnings, not waiting for God's movements to gain momentum. Satan is a religionist who has missionaries able to attract and to hold some of the mighty of earth. Satan is not afraid of religion, but is afraid of salvation, and he fights bitterly the preaching of the Gospel. He is wily but not wise. The Holy Spirit is the Spirit of Wisdom, as well as the Spirit of Truth.

THE SERMON

BEATING THE DEVIL AT HIS OWN GAME.

Acts 13: 6-13.

A STUDY of the devil, his ways and his wiles would be a very profitable occupation for many, these days. Next to knowing the Lord Jesus Christ in saving and keeping power, the child of God should know about the devil and how to meet his onslaughts. The Apostle Paul declared that Christians were not ignorant of his wiles.

"Oh," I hear some one saying, "I don't believe in a personal devil." I remember reading some years ago a statement by the late Elbert Hubbard: "He who believes in a personal devil *is* one"; but, in the interest of truth, I should say that, he that doesn't believe in a personal devil is in his service.

An unfailing test for finding out the reality of the devil is to serve God whole-heartedly and oppose the wickedness of the Evil One. Then you will know. Of course, there are some folks who don't believe in that. They don't believe in opposing the devil because they dislike family quarrels. Some churches don't even mention his name, and, when that is true, they're not doing much opposition to his work. Talk about battling the devil! I suppose that a third of the churches never throw even so much as a custard pie into his territory.

We have a very profitable study before us in the record of the conversion of Sergius Paulus, and the defeat of Elymas, the sorcerer, and, as we proceed with the story, we shall note the following lessons it contains.

I. The Devil Sees to It That His Emissaries Are Busy Where God's Messengers Are at Work.

Let us note the drama of the situation. The church at Antioch was sending out its first missionaries. Paul was starting out on his great missionary career. The Holy Ghost was directing the affair. No wonder the devil got busy; it was high time. You know the devil is lots wiser than some of the children of light. He knows the necessity of resisting beginnings. The Church of God and the individual Christian is usually asleep at the beginnings of evil, and only when the wicked come in like a flood, and an overwhelming flood at that, do they become alive to the situation. Were it not for the protectiveness of God and His almighty power, the Christian Church and the individual Christian would have been wiped out of existence long ago. The devil knows how hard it is to stop a movement once it has gained momentum. The Christian can expect the devil to make a supreme effort to down him the moment he starts out in the service of God.

As we have a drama here, we had better note the *cast of characters*. There is Barnabas, a great, noble soul and a devout Christian. There is Saul, now Paul, the greatest preacher and missionary of all time. There is John Mark, used of God in writing the second Gospel. There is Sergius Paulus, a Roman deputy, whom both God and Satan wanted. There is Elymas, the devil's instrument, a sorcerer, whose real name was Barjesus (meaning "son of Joshua"), a bad man with a good name. A literal rendering of his name would be, "the son of Jehovah's salvation"; yet he was a child of the devil! I always hate to see a man with a good name in a bad business—don't you?

Now, let us look at the *stage,* itself. The battle is in the devil's territory. Paphos was a wicked pagan city. It was called the City of Aphrodite. There was there an ancient temple erected to the worship of Venus. Now Venus was the goddess of sensuality, and we are told that the practices connected with this temple were abominable. It is well to remember that the devil always prospers where sensuality abounds. Not that he is necessarily the author of sensuality, because that is one of the sins of the flesh; but sensuality is one of the most deadening of sins. Gross participation in the lusts of the flesh soon deadens every finer sensibility; not only is the body steeped in degeneracy, but the soul itself is drugged and stupefied to the finer things of life, and therefore comparatively senseless to the Gospel.

The Bible reveals that where sensuality has prevailed for a long while, the only thing that can cure it is a severe judgment from God. Witness Babylon— witness Nineveh—witness Sodom and Gomorrah. How long God will withhold His judging hand on our own civilization, especially our own country with its nudity, its lewdness, its licentiousness and sin, no one can prophesy; but we can declare that God will not withhold His judging hand forever. Our theatres, our motion pictures, our magazines, our books, and pictures, are all catering to this sensuousness. It disgusts me when I hear New Yorkers boast about the glory of Times Square and the lights of Broadway. Don't boast; hang your head in shame, for the world has probably not produced, anywhere, another such cesspool of sensuousness and sin as that which can be found on Broadway at Forty-second Street and its environment. A sensitive, spiritual soul can almost smell the devil as he walks through that territory.

Yes, a sensuous age is an age in which the devil thrives, because he finds men and women mentally and morally depleted and spiritually deadened, and they become an easy prey of his wiles.

II. God Has His Needy Ones Where His Messengers Work.

We now take a closer look at Sergius Paulus. He was a *prominent man*, he was the proconsul and governor of Cyprus, and it is suggested that he was an extraordinarily intelligent man—something of a philosopher. One may well imagine that he supposed he was doing Paul a great favor when this apostle and Barnabas came to his community and were received by him. In reality, however, the favor was being done him. It was a great favor that God should visit him with salvation.

We are told, also, that he was *prudent*—that is, a thinking, intelligent man, and when we ponder this we are brought to realize that Elymas was not just a cheap fortune teller. This sorcerer was a clever religionist; he undoubtedly had an intellectual approach to the faith he propagated. He could never have appealed to Sergius with any cheap legerdemain.

Please remember the devil is never afraid of religion; that's his specialty! But he is wholesomely afraid of salvation. Many wonder why it is that modernism makes its appeal so often to the intellectuals. The answer to that is that the pride of human intellect despises the Gospel. The Word of God has said that not many wise, not many mighty, not many noble, are called, and it declares also that the natural man perceiveth not the things of God for they are foolishness unto him. Neither can he understand them because they are spiritually discerned. Modernism is essentially the religion of the natural man; it is the religion of the proud human heart. The Gospel breaks down the barriers of pride, and brings a man penitently to the foot of the Cross. Human learning does not relish this sort of thing; but it is well to remember that human knowledge cannot keep any man from being fooled by the devil. The wiser he is the harder he falls!

On the other hand, the thinking man may not be very far from the kingdom. God does not discourage thought upon the matter of faith. As a matter of fact, He encourages it. His unmistakable declaration is "Come, now, let us reason together." The emphasis is not only upon the word "reason," but upon the word "together." The trouble with the intellectual rejecting the Gospel is that he reasons apart from God. If he'd bring his reasoning into cooperation with God's revelation, there would be no difficulty about the matter. A little sane reasoning would show any man that he is a lost sinner, and needs a Saviour; and a little reason applied to the study of revelation would show him that the Gospel and its working is an enevitable thing, and, although supernatural in its nature, is in its application a natural thing. Any reasonable person should know that until he is right with God through faith in Jesus Christ, he is not right with himself or with anybody else.

God evidently knew that Sergius was worth getting for the kingdom. The devil knew it, also, and wanted him badly. We must not be respecters of persons in our saving ministry, but it is not unchristian to covet the leadership of our day for Jesus Christ. I seldom hear a great singer on the radio with a voice that captivates the hearts of people without wishing that perhaps he might yield his heart to Jesus Christ and sing the Gospel in the power of the Spirit. What a blessing he could be and what a power for God. I never read the stories of such opposers of the truth as Ingersoll, Darrow and others, with their brilliant minds and ability to move the public, without thinking of what they might have done for God had they known Jesus Christ in a saving way and been dedicated to Him.

I've been thinking, recently, of Leon Trotsky. Oh, the earnestness and enthusiasm of the man! Irrepressible and effervescent, hounded from one country to another, yet never giving up his philosophy, nor failing to preach his gospel, as damnable as it is; and I recall that, years ago, Leon Trotsky, as a Jew named Bronstein, lived in New York's lower East Side, in this

nominally Christian country of ours, under the sound
of the church bells of this great city, and, humanly
speaking, he might have been reached for Christ. What
a power he would have been—a veritable second Paul!
But the devil got him and a million Christians were
bathed in their own blood, in Russia. The greatest on-
slaught against the faith in modern times emanates from
the philosophy which he has espoused and which he
propagated with every ounce of his wondrous energy.

III. SATAN IS WILY BUT NOT WISE.

The battle continues, the plot thickens, and Elymas
launches to the attack. The text seems rather passive.
It states merely that Elymas withstood the preaching
of Paul and Barnabas, endeavoring to turn the Deputy
from the faith; but, if we read between the lines, we
learn that the conflict was intense. This false prophet
doubtless interfered with a view to preventing his
master from yielding to the Apostle's preaching and
of deadening its influence upon Sergius Paulus. Farrar
declares that probably he spared neither argument nor
insult in his endeavor to persuade Sergius of the ab-
surdity of the new faith. He may have reviled Christ
as a crucified malefactor, and denounced Him as an
enemy of Moses. Ridicule and satire is often used
as an effective weapon by the devil.

If any attack were made on the person of Christ,
it would not have been surprising to see the Holy
Ghost entering the lists, and we read the startling statement in the ninth verse: "Then Saul (who is also called
Paul), filled with the Holy Ghost, set his eyes on him,

and said, O full of all subtlety and all mischief, thou
child of the devil, thou enemy of all righteousness, wilt
thou not cease to pervert the right ways of the Lord?"
What a denunciation! Elymas is accused of three
things: having craft and cunning, being a child of the
devil, and an enemy of righteousness.

The question that comes to our minds immediately
is, was not Paul unduly harsh? Surely he was un-
Christlike here. Some tender souls would declare that
he should have been a little more charitable. But the
difficulty of such reasoning is that we don't know Christ.
The world and the Church, in some instances, have
been propagating a false Christ, or, perhaps to be more
exact, a "half-Christ"; they have been presenting a
Christ of tenderness and sympathy, and have failed to
remember His rugged anger and uncompromising denunciation of sin and evil. It would pay us periodically
to read the woes pronounced upon the Pharisees and
learn that love can be awful in judgment, as well as
tender in compassion.

But the truth is that there is no room for human
speculation concerning this matter. In reality, it is
not Paul who speaks, but the Holy Ghost. This is not
a flare of human passion; it is a demonstration of divine indignation. This is not the contentious accusation
of an embittered man, but the righteous denunciation
of a Holy God through His messenger; and, what is
more, there is no element of slander here. Remember
that Paul told Elymas to his face, and did not rail
at him behind his back.

Oh, that we might have such holy men and such

uncompromising denunciation today! We have no little sarcasm and no small amount of innuendo, but this is Holy Ghost-directed condemnation. The solemn truth is, that no man has a right to take the weapon of condemnation in the flesh. Too much of the preachers' condemnation is done in the energy of the flesh. The result is wounds that are infected and will not heal; but when the Holy Ghost is present, directing operations, the servant of God may swing the sword and every wound made will be cauterized and evil will be sloughed off with every fell swoop; but so little is done in this direction we are forced to agree with Joseph Parker when he says: "We have lost our fire to-day; we talk to Elymas, not in syllables of fire as did the Apostles, but in syllables of ice."

As I walk about the streets of this city and see the sin, godlessness, and indifference, a cry comes up in my soul and a great longing in my heart that some one might really be raised up of God to speak in the power of the Holy Ghost; one able to condemn the awful sin and licentiousness of this city, and bring multitudes to repentance at the foot of the Cross.

Because of Paul's faithfulness and boldness in the Spirit, the devil was defeated, and the way is paved for God to manifest His glory in the whole affair. Elymas is stricken blind in condemnation, Sergius Paulus is convicted and saved; there is darkness for Elymas and light for Paulus.

By the way, this is Paul's first recorded miracle, and we feel sure that the judgment was not of his own doing but divinely directed, because Paul had suffered too much of blindness himself, at his conversion, to ever use that as an instrument of judgment upon others of his own free will.

Rather harsh, you say; yes, God *does* destroy, as well as make alive; God has a hell as well as a heaven. He sets His love upon men, He plans for their redemption, and woe unto that person who attempts to thwart the plan of God.

I am told that a railroad line between Cripple Creek and Colorado Springs drops more than four thousand feet in a distance of forty miles. All along this line are signs marked "derailing switch." The reason for the multiplicity of derailing switches, we are told, is so that, if an engine loses control and runs wild, it can be plunged against the side of the mountain, and destroyed, before it destroys other trains and lives.

Now, God also has some derailing switches. Individuals that stand in His way persistently and unrepentantly, are put out of the way, in order that souls might be saved. All along the track of history God has had these derailing switches, into which individuals, cities, and nations that have lost control of themselves and become instruments of the devil and menaces to the world have been thrown, and we praise God for this action on His part.

But was Elymas ever saved? There is no record that he was, and, if he was a true apostate, he never found salvation; but, of course, there is a question as to that. But whether Elymas was saved or not, this much is true, that *you* may be saved. You are the object of God's mercy, you are the subject of His re-

deeming love. If it were possible for Elymas to be
saved (and we may well suppose that it was) what
a calamity that he should be so near to the power of
God and His grace and yet fail to appropriate it!
The term Elymas means "the wise," but think of his
lack of wisdom! The Word of God says that the fear
of the Lord is the beginning of wisdom, and that fear
means reverential, and not cringing fear. Yes, my
brother, there's hope for you, and may God help you
to find Him who is your salvation and your eternal
hope.

> *Not far, not far from the Kingdom,*
>   *Yet in the shadow of sin;*
> *How many are coming and going!—*
>   *How few there are entering in!*
>
> *Not far, not far from the Kingdom,*
>   *Where voices whisper and wait;*
> *Too timid to enter in boldly,*
>   *So linger still outside the gate.*
>
> *Away in the dark and the danger,*
>   *Far out in the night and the cold;*
> *There Jesus is waiting to lead you*
>   *So tenderly into His fold.*
>
> *Not far, not far from the Kingdom,*
>   *'Tis only a little space;*
> *But oh, you may still be for ever*
>   *Shut out from yon heavenly place!*

V.

THE CONVERSION OF LYDIA

Acts 16: 12-15.

THE STUDY

The Occasion.

PAUL AND Silas come to Philippi on the Apostle's second missionary journey in response to Paul's vision of the pleading man of Macedonia. They had been directed by the Holy Spirit to evangelize Europe through the fact that the Spirit forbade them to preach the Word in Asia. Having looked around for a place to begin operations in Philippi, they are directed to a prayer meeting outside the city by a riverside. There they find a handful of devout women. Quietly, they sit down with them to tell them the story of the Gospel.

The Subject.

Lydia, an Asiatic business woman, a seller of purple cloth from Thyatira, is the first, if not the only convert of the group. She may have been a Jewish proselyte, or even a true Jew, though her name belies this. At any rate, she was devout enough to close up her business in a pagan city and find her place on the Jewish Sabbath with those who loved to pray.

75

The Agent.

Paul here does a definite and successful piece of individual soul winning. Of course, God had opened Lydia's heart.

The Accompaniment.

Everything is quiet in this conversion, neither man nor devil seeming to oppose. We wonder if the devil is caught napping in this affair, since we note he is very angry a little later when the evil spirit is cast out of the soothsaying damsel. The quiet effectiveness of Spirit-directed personal work is seen here.

The Results.

The results of Lydia's conversion are far-reaching. Her heart was opened and she became a Christian. Her home was opened and became a church. The heart of Lydia became a doorway for a revival in Philippi, and for the evangelization of Europe.

Significant Lessons.

God's greatest movements start from insignificant beginnings, most times. The evangelization of Europe started in a prayer meeting, and not at a banquet. The Church, to-day, is starting too many things by sitting down to eat instead of kneeling down to pray. The man of Macedonia turned out to be a woman. God alone knows the possibilities of a woman's life saved and consecrated to Him. Here, again, is God's directing grace choosing outstanding leadership.

THE SERMON

THE SALVATION OF WOMANHOOD—OR WHEN A WOMAN BELIEVES

Acts 16: 12-15.

A LITTLE coast-plying vessel is sailing at a merry clip directly before a brisk summer breeze blowing westward across the historic Aegean Sea from the sunny shores of Asia Minor. Among the motley group of passengers on board are four men bound on a very uncertain mission.

The leader of the group is a small bearded figure who would be a nondescript individual were it not for his magnificent head, and the rather sad, far-away look in his eyes—the attitude of one who seems to see things beyond the horizon. He is unmistakably a Jew, but his quiet dignity tells of culture and refinement which is Grecian. He is so at ease in the jostling, jabbering crowd on the little coast vessel that we are compelled to note a mien of self-resignation which approximates a beauty nearly heavenly. This man's name is Paul.

With him are three other travelers of like quiet earnestness. One is a young man, tall and of fine face, with keen eyes and athletic bearing. His friends call him Timotheus. We hear them call another by the name of Silas. He is less attractive; is older, but his face is kind and earnest.

The fourth figure is by far the most outstanding of the group. His is the face of a scholar, features finely moulded and Grecian in character. He has the quiet, unperturbed attitude of the scientist. His speech is exquisite, and his voice resonant. This is Luke, the physician.

But the first man is obviously the leader of the group, and the others wait respectfully on his word.

The ship lands at Neapolis, and the quartet disembark and make their way completely through the city and out into the country on one of the solid Roman roads that winds north and west to the thriving bustling city of Philippi, the chief metropolis of Macedonia in Greece. On they go, through the busy streets, this little man and his three companions, unnoticed by the populace, and find a little inn where they are lodged inexpensively.

As far as that city was concerned, these men were unheralded and unsung, and their presence caused not a ripple. What was the arrival of four harmless travelers to the doings of the mighty Roman Empire in that day? Yet the coming of Paul and his companions to Philippi was of greater importance to that city and of greater moment to the whole world than the conquests of the great King Philip, after whom the city had been named.

Now what had brought them on this journey? A whole chain of events had entered in. Some of them were natural, others supernatural. It was Paul's second missionary journey. Nearly twenty years before, he had found Christ on the Damascus Road. Nearly a decade had elapsed since the church at Antioch had sent Barnabas and him out as their special missionaries.

Strong churches had been established throughout Asia Minor, and Syria, and Paul had desired to continue his work down into Asia—the millions of India and China and the isles of the sea, perhaps were claiming his attention—but the Spirit forbade this.

Then came a vision at Troas; a man of Macedonia appeared to Paul in the night, a man standing and praying him saying, "Come over into Macedonia and help us!" This vision made a tremendous impression upon Paul, and after counsel with his friends they decided that the vision was the call of the Lord to Macedonia and, the direction of the Spirit into Europe, and the passing of the Gospel to the west. "Westward the course of empire takes its way," wrote Bishop Berkley, many centuries after this event, but the beginnings of the westward march of the Gospel are seen here.

If they felt that God was going to give them a hilarious reception because of the vision, they were gravely mistaken, and when they got to Philippi they found no welcoming committee. Sadder still, they found practically no religious life in the city. There was no synagogue there, and, if there had been ten male Jews of prominence, there could have been a synagogue, and doubtless would have been.

On the contrary, religious meetings were apparently not permitted in the city, and all semblance of religious life had to be carried on outside its environs. So out by a riverside, where prayer was permitted to be made, these men find a number of devout women, and they sit down with them and tell them the story of the Gospel.

I never read this story without wondering where the men were. Surely there must have been some devout men, but, if there were any, they were in an apostate condition and, probably, out playing golf, or whatever was its gaming equivalent in that day. Oh, the faithfulness of womanhood! God alone knows where we might be were it not for the faithfulness of womankind. Womanhood has done much for the Gospel, but the Gospel also has done much for womanhood. The very fact that Paul was sitting down with a group of women and telling the simple story shows the power of the Gospel, for Paul in his Jewish days, or perhaps better to say his Judaistic days, as a strict Pharisee had ofttimes repeated the Pharisee's prayer: "Oh God, I thank thee that I am neither a Gentile, nor a slave, nor a woman." But the Lord Jesus had taught him to say that in Christ is neither bond nor free, neither male nor female, Jew nor Gentile, but Christ is all and in all.

Now, according to the story, they had at least one convert. Her name was Lydia, and her we study here.

I. Some Facts Concerning This Woman.

She was a business woman—a seller of purple from the city of Thyatira. As we read this story, it seems that we are dealing with an up-to-date matter. Women in business seems to be a very modern idea, but apparently some of them were in business back in New Testament times. Of course, they were in the minority, these business women, but, to-day, womanhood has entered every door of the business field, and there's not a vocation which she does not occupy.

Doubtless Lydia had many of the outward manifestations of genuine leadership; she was an exceptional business woman, and there are indications that she was rich. The Apostle Paul, with his eager mind and spirit and keen eye for leadership, would very readily be attracted to her. Not that the Apostle worshipped wealth, but he *did* appreciate worth. The Church should never bow to the domination of the dollar, but it should acquiesce to the possibilities of Christian leadership in those who have made a success in the field of business.

Lydia was a consecrated business woman. A Gentile woman, doubtless, but perhaps a Jewish proselyte, one of the "God-fearers" of that time, like Cornelius. Her consecration is evidenced by the fact that she was glad to shut up shop in the pagan city on the Jewish Sabbath and go out with this small group and worship God. Truly, this is proof of the genuineness of her faith. Every devout soul, it seems, instinctively recognizes the necessity of one day in seven given over to worship. Any violation of this rule is hypocrisy and means spiritual death.

I read some time ago of a little boy who came to his mother with a very worried question. "Mamma," the boy said, "I'm awfully afraid that Daddy won't ever get to heaven." With a look of surprise, the mother said, "Why, son, why do you say that? Your Daddy believes in God and is a Christian. What do you think will keep him out of heaven?" "Well," replied the lad, "Daddy seems so busy all the time, he can't leave the store to play with me, and he can't leave the store to go to church, and he can't leave the store to go to prayer meeting; so I am afraid he won't be able to leave the store to go to heaven."

Too much of business is infected with this awful disease that, of itself, seems so harmless because it is merely negative, but which is deadly in reality; but we are thankful to note that this woman did not allow her business life to interfere with her obligations to God.

It has been my joy to know a great number of business women as church members, and almost all of them if they were good business women, were also faithful Christians. Not only did I find them faithful to the service of the church, but faithful to the tasks that were given them; but another and very important factor of their lives was that, in practically every case, I discovered them to be generous givers to the work of the church and the Kingdom of God. Many of them were businesslike in their dealings with God, and were tithers and faithful in their tenth. Oh, for more folks who have religion in their business, and who put business into their religion.

But there are other kinds of women in business, and what a detriment to society they have made of themselves. They work like men, they work with men. They sin like men, and they sin with men; and no small part of the degradation of the lost morals of our day comes from the fact that women, forced to leave their homes because of economic and social conditions, have gone into business with men and have lowered their standards in moral things.

Men do not like women to be their equal; especially, they do not like them to be their equal in immorality. Men desire to put women on a pedestal, and, unfortunately, the intermingling of men and women in business and in factories has lowered the standard and has lowered male appreciation, and chivalry is all but gone from the race.

Every hard working business woman needs diversion, especially religious diversion. Many seek happiness in a career, and think that success will bring peace and blessings; but Jenny Lind at the height of her career and popularity in America realized this to be false. She said once to a friend that her experience was that of the poet:—

"In vain I seek for rest in all created good,
It leaves me still unblessed and makes me cry
for God."

Business women may find just the relief they desire in the work of the church and the kingdom of God, and we may truthfully say that the whole cause of Christ would have gone under a thousand times but for faithful womanhood, for the manhood of the church has ofttimes been very spasmodic in its efforts and faithfulness; but womanhood has kept the fires of morals and spirituality alight by prayer, by faithful attendance upon the house of God, and by faithful participation in the work of the Kingdom of God.

Lydia was a woman spiritually prepared. Dr.

Clovis Chappell suggests: "Little did Lydia dream that Sabbath morning that she was going to a place that would make her name remembered when the empire of the Caesars had vanished from the centuries. She did not know that anything out of the ordinary would take place. But, because she thought it was her duty and because she needed heart help, she went to this prayer meeting that was held by the riverside under the open sky. She was living up to the best she knew, she was using all the light that God had granted her. This made it possible for Him to lead her into the fullness of the light."

God had opened Lydia's heart; she gave heed to the preaching. Paul found his beginning in Europe in her. Ah, God knows his servants, God knows how to start a revival. If only we would seek to do His will explicitly, what blessing God would do. God knows what He wants done, and He knows just who He has to do it.

II. THE BLESSED RESULTS OF HER CONVERSION.

Her heart became a doorway. This is typical of womankind—oh, the thousands that God has used in this same way! When a woman's heart is surrendered to God, I've noted from observation that God loves to come trooping through it to bless multitudes. The heart of a redeemed woman seems to be so full of wonderful possibilities.

Lydia's heart was a doorway for the truth. We read that she accepted Christ and was baptized. A man of

Macedonia summoned Paul to Europe, but, true to
experience, a woman received him; or, as some one
has put it, the man of Macedonia turned out finally
to be a woman. She not only received God into her
heart, but she received Paul and his message and the
things of Christianity into her life.

Lydia became a doorway to a city church. Her
home was opened as well as her heart. Give me a
Christian woman and I'll guarantee soon to have a
Christian home, and where there's a Christian home
there's bound to be Christian men and Christian influence.

It is worthy of note that although a business woman,
Lydia had a home which, doubtless, was her especial
sphere of influence. This proves that she had the true
womanly instinct. We are told that after she was baptized she besought the disciples, saying, "If ye have
judged me to be faithful to the Lord, come into my
house, and abide there." Oh, the blessing of the old
hospitable homes of other days! Some of them still
remain, of course, and many of you were raised in
such an one, where they entertained the ministers and
the missionaries. Some remember hearing the preval-
ent joke declaring: "There were 'locust preachers
buzzing around and eating everything in sight,' and
they made some of the children wait to eat at the second table," but nevertheless they were a blessing to your
home and their very presence there proved that goodness was paramount.

In Lydia's home a church was established, one of
the greatest in Europe; Paul always loved it, and when

you read his epistles to the Philippians you will find
that his heart goes out in tenderness and sympathy to
the Christians that were gathered in that city and to
the little church that began with the conversion of
Lydia and the hospitality of her home.

Lydia became the doorway for great revival. The
work in Philippi, the work in Europe, started in a
prayer meeting. Very significant. I am becoming in-
creasingly suspicious of religious meetings that start
with a banquet; that's the way the world accomplishes
things, and God never does things in a worldly way.
History is without a single example of a great religious
movement that ever started with a meal, because, in that
way, we begin with the flesh and end therewith. Great
religious movements begin with a great heart-yearning,
and then God finishes the task. We inaugurate too much
within the church, today, by sitting down to eat, when
we ought to be kneeling down to pray.

Many stories are told of the beginning of the great
Welsh revival in the early years of the century; but
the most likely story is that connected with a lone
watcher and wanderer over the Welsh hills. Day after
day this man was seen walking along the mountain
pathways, finding secluded spots for prayer. Day after
day, week after week, month after month, he agonized.
But suddenly he was gone. The neighborhood saw him
no more; the prayer had ended, evidently, but the work
of God had not ended. Suddenly in a little church in
a Welsh village, a little maid got up and simply testified to her faith in Christ and to the blessing that God
had brought to her life. It was but a wisp of flame, but

suddenly it began to catch and to unite with other wisps of flame, and soon a great revival was sweeping over Wales, with a power and a blessing unequaled since the days of the Apostles. In too many instances, to-day, we make prayer a sort of sanctimonious coat of paint for the house of our selfish endeavor; when prayer is not anything superficial, it is fundamental. We should lay prayer down as a foundation, then build the house of our achievement upon it as a basis.

Lydia's heart was a doorway for the conversion of Europe. Lydia herself was not a European, but an Asiatic; her home was not in Philippi but in Thyatira; she merely was in Philippi on business, though she may have maintained a temporary home there. But through her the Gospel got a foothold. If you will read on in this story, you will discover that, with Lydia, Paul got a start for the Gospel in Europe. Then under the power and direction of the Spirit of God he strikes at every centre of civilization, Thessalonica, Athens, Corinth, finally Rome itself, and all through the doorway of this woman's heart.

III. Lydia's Life Is a Challenge to Modern Womanhood.

A challenge to salvation. Womanhood is God's workshop in nature, and ofttimes she is his chief instrument in grace. Oh, how the world needs consecrated women in this dark hour. Oh womanhood, that listens to my voice, in God's name be saved, and be used of Him.

Lydia is a challenge to faithful living. Womanhood, to-day, in too many instances is leaving her first estate, that of a helpmeet to the man and becoming his plaything. Shall womanhood sell its high birthright on the altar of our sensuous, senseless age? Listen, womanhood! Into your arms God has placed the race at its beginning. As a mother your influence is prenatal and, in spite of all the institutions that come into the life of your child, God gives that child to you when it is plastic and when your life and your influence and your prayers can etch in delicate tracery the lines that will in later life develop into the strong delineations of character. What a trust is yours; what an incentive to faithful living!

Lydia is a challenge to all mothers' sons and daughters. Think what you owe to-night to mothers, to sisters, to other godly women. As I look back at my own experience in the Christian life, and realize how prominent a place womanhood played in my conversion, I am astounded. My own mother prayed for me, gave me to the Lord at birth, and although she died when I was just past five years of age, eighteen years after she was in her grave, I found the Lord. She gave me to the ministry, and God called me into His service. During the Billy Sunday campaign in Boston, I was led to a saving knowledge of Christ as a result of two forces; first the prayers of my sister, who had recently been led to Christ by the pastor's assistant at Clarendon Street Baptist Church, who was a woman graduate of the Moody Bible Institute, and who joined with my sister in a covenant of prayer for my salvation, and the first one to talk to me about my soul was a little woman in the Tabernacle in Boston, who put her hand upon my shoulder and said, "Young man, don't you want to be a Christian?"

Oh, beloved, if we were to take away the influence of womanhood upon our lives how many of us would ever reach heaven? The percentage would indeed be small.

In a sermon delivered in the chapel of Mansfield College, Oxford, Dr. Selbie told this daring story. There was a young Frenchman who loved a courtesan. This woman hated her lover's mother. When, in his passion, he offered her any gift in return for her love, she answered: "Bring me your mother's bleeding heart." In his madness, this young man went to his home and killed his mother, and plucking out her heart, hurried by night through the streets, carrying it to the cruel woman to whom he had given his soul. But as he went he stumbled and fell, and from the bleeding heart came an anxious voice, "Son, are you hurt?" Not even murder could kill that mother's love. It lived on in the torn heart.

Just a fable, of course, but true in sentiment and true to experience. When the records of heaven are opened to our redeemed eyes, what a story we shall read of sacrificial womanhood, whose hearts the Lord had opened and through whose hearts the forces of righteousness came trooping to the blessing of the multitude!

"Oh Mother when I think of thee
'Tis but a step to Calvary.
Thy precious hand upon my brow
Is leading me to Jesus now."

VI.

THE CONVERSION OF THE PHILIPPIAN JAILER

THE STUDY

Acts 16: 25-34.

The Occasion.

THE STORY begins with the damsel who was possessed with a spirit of divination, and whose masters had gained much by her soothsaying. Because of her following the Apostles and crying, "These men are the servants of the most high God, which shew unto us the way of salvation," Paul is grieved and says in the Spirit and to the spirit, "I command thee in the name of Jesus Christ, to come out of her." And he came out the same hour. The masters, seeing that their greed of gain was gone, had Paul and Silas hurried before the magistrate. There was no semblance of a legal trial, but merely condemnation. The Apostles are beaten and jailed in the innermost dungeon, with their feet in the stocks. Then comes the earthquake and deliverance. Here is conversion under uproarious and supernatural circumstances. The unexpected is predominant here.

The Subject.

This Philippian Jailer is evidently a semi-ignorant Roman soldier, hardened in brutality. His adverse treatment of Paul and Silas was not by order, but by choice.

The Agent.

Paul and Silas and supernatural accompaniments are at work here.

The Accompaniment.

Here we have salvation coming out of pandemonium, lawlessness, brutality, and nature's upheaval; yet peaceful, trusting, and praiseful servants in the midst of the bedlam are found. Physical fear is the major emotion of the Jailer. His question, "Lords, what must I do to be saved?" is not an evangelical one, but Paul makes it so by his reply. There is true penitence found in the attitude of the Jailer.

Results.

The salvation of the Jailer and his family with rejoicing and a testimony which scared the magistrates, seem to be the major result of this conversion.

Significant Lessons.

Peacefulness and patience under unjust persecution is a condition which God can mightily use. The essential passion of Paul's soul is seen in this quick turn of the Jailer's question to the thought of personal salvation. "All God's chillun's got a song," including a song in the night!

THE SERMON

GOD'S GREAT JAIL DELIVERY—OR PRAYED OUT OF PRISON.

Acts 16: 25-34.

WE WERE somewhat surprised in the study of the conversion of Lydia at Philippi to discover that there

was no opposition, either by man or devil, and we had
wondered if the devil had been caught napping; but
if he had, we discover that he is wide awake again, as
we face the situation that comes before us now.

As Paul and his companions continued their work
in Philippi, a certain damsel possessed with a spirit
of divination met them, a girl who had been used by
her masters through her demon-possessed character for
soothsaying purposes. She possessed literally the spirit
of a python. Now we are told that the serpent which
guarded the Delphi prophetess was a python, and therefore we appear to have here a prophetic demon pos-
sessing the girl. Unprincipled men had discovered that
this poor girl was profitable, and a sort of stock company had been formed in her and her soothsaying business, and they took her about from place to place, and
had her speak under the power of this demon and
collected money for the supposed prophecies which she
made. She probably did little more than give off a
few insane ravings most of the time, but it was different
when she came into contact with Paul and Silas.

Demons ordinarily haven't much sense. I have
never been able to see why folks would take up spirit-
ism; why they would believe that their loved ones had
nothing better to do in the after-life than to come back
to earth, blow horns, and tip over tables, and rap on
doors, and do all sorts of queer things which the spirit-
ists claim that they do. But when you have a case of
genuine demon possession, and when it's brought face
to face with the truth of God, you may get some truth.
It will be recalled that demons confessed that Jesus

Christ was the Son of God when He was upon earth, and He silenced them, and in this case the demon recognized that Paul and Silas were the servants of the most high God. But the Gospel wants no testimony from demons, only from the redeemed, and Paul is grieved and rebukes the spirit and exorcises the demon out of the girl. Elymas, the sorcerer, about whom we studied in the conversion of Sergius Paulus, was voluntarily and wilfully a child of the devil; but here was a poor slave girl who was involuntarily possessed. It is worthy of our attention to study these two types of individuals in their relationship to demon possession.

The profits of her masters gone, they trump up false charges against Paul and Silas and hurry them off to the magistrate, where they are judged according to the popular cry, not according to law and testimony. Then follows a beating, imprisonment and songs of deliverance.

I. TRUE CHRISTIANITY IS A TROUBLE-MAKING RELIGION.

Though it brings peace to the individual heart, it certainly does bring trouble into the world whenever it interferes with sin or gain, which it is likely to do.

The hue and cry is ofttimes raised that we should keep religion out of politics, or politics out of religion, but, in the main, this is an impossibility, because both deal with men and morals, and function in the same areas, and when politics is corrupt and religion is true there is bound to be a collision. To-day, the Church must speak out against greed and must never bow to the bossism and mercenariness of the times, which are so afraid that the sermon will hit the pocketbook.

Religion is tolerated by godless communities so long as it does not interfere with sin or gain. There doubtless was nothing more than a little ridicule over the conversion of Lydia, but when an evil spirit was cast out of a certain girl, and her soothsaying ability was lost and pocketbooks were touched and Satan's lordship disputed, there was trouble on hand. Now, there are two great sources of trouble in the work of the Kingdom of God. First, "bossism," when there is a limiting of power and authority to those accustomed to rule; and, second, from mercenariness, when there is the hitting of the sins that affect the pocketbook. Jesus ran afoul the first, and Paul was persecuted for the second.

Christianity causes trouble when it demands consistent living. The Church of God should be hated by the ungodly, not laughed at for its inconsistency, but hated for its righteousness and opposition to all evil.

II. CHRISTIANITY IS A RELIGION OF SUFFERING.

Outwardly, we have trouble predominating here. God ofttimes brings blessing out of trouble. Sometimes He must send disaster or threaten doom before He can bring men's hearts to the place of surrender. He longs to lead us without bit and bridle, as He says through the Psalmist, but sometimes we're "mulish" and He has to put the bit in our mouths and yank us back on our haunches before we look up into His face.

On one occasion Sir Harry Lauder told of the tragedy that came into his life when his only boy was killed in the trenches in France. Stark tragedy stared him squarely in the face. "I found before me three possible ways of escape," said the Scottish songster, "one was drink; I could drown my sorrow in a continuous debauch of alcohol, but I felt that that would not do. The second was suicide; I could take my life and hide myself in the grave from my sorrow, but my training and religious background did not permit *that*. Then, there was God; casting all my care upon Him, letting Him help me out of my trouble and comfort me in my sorrow. "And," says Sir Harry, "I found God."

Too many people come to religious faith thinking that thereafter everything will be ease and lethargy, but these Apostles did not find it so. They had had a glorious vision and the Macedonian call to come over into Europe and help with the Gospel; and the result was imprisonment and beating and suffering unspeakable; and yet you could not discourage them. They counted it a privilege to suffer for Jesus Christ. One is reminded of the poem by Annie Johnson Flint*:

> *Oh, there's many a thorn on the Jesus way,*
> *   Many a thorn I know,*
> *There is grief and loss and the pain of the Cross,*
> *   Wherever my feet may go,*
> *But the Lord will heal all the wounds I bear,*
> *   When the thorns have pricked me sore,*
> *For He's planted a rose where the briar grows,*
> *   And He's walked this way before.*

Oh, there's many a storm on the Jesus way,
  Many a storm I see,
And the night is black and the wind's wild rack
  Throws angry waves over me,
But the Lord Himself is in my little ship,
  And the winds obey His will,
By the word He has said "Be ye not afraid,"
  My heart and the waves grow still.

Oh, there's many a foe on the Jesus way,
  Many a foe to fight,
And all the day I must watch and pray,
  In keeping my armor bright,
But the Lord is ever at my right hand,
  The Tempter's wiles to meet,
Though the foe may be strong and the fight be long,
  He shall never know defeat.

III. CHRISTIANITY IS A RELIGION OF SONG.

The fortitude and irrepressible faith of the Apostles is seen by the fact that deep in the dungeon, with their feet fast in the stocks, and their backs bleeding and paining excruciatingly, they could still sing songs of praises unto God. What a glorious song it must have been, sung there in the midst of the filthy and foul dungeon. How the Spirit must have helped their infirmities! Truly, "all God's chillun" have got a song! One is reminded of Madame Guyon's lines, written while in prison:

---

*"From 'By The Way or Travelogues of Cheer' by Annie Johnson Flint, published and copyrighted by Evangelical Publishers, Toronto, Canada."

A little bird am I,
  Shut from the fields and air,
And in my cage I sit and sing,
  To Him who placed me there,
Well pleased a prisoner to be,
Because, my God, it pleases thee.

Naught have I else to do,
  I sing the whole day long,
And He whom most I love to please,
  Doth listen to my song.
He caught and bound my wandering wing,
But still He bends to hear me sing.

My cage confines me round,
  Abroad I cannot fly,
But though my wing is closely bound,
  My heart's at liberty,
My prison walls cannot control,
The flight, the freedom of the soul.

Oh, it is good to soar
  These bolts and bars above
To Him whose purpose I adore,
  Whose providence I love,
And in Thy mighty will to find,
The joy, the freedom of the mind.

Yes, Christianity is a religion of song. Blind unbelief, black atheism, has little to sing about, but "all

God's chillun got a song," a song for all ages and conditions of life.

There is a song for babyhood, and the little ones
can lisp:

> *"Jesus loves me, this I know,*
> *For the Bible tells me so."*

And at Christmas time their baby voices are heard
singing:

> *"Away in a manger, no crib for His bed,*
> *The little Lord Jesus, laid down His sweet head."*

There is a song for the convert, newly born. He
can stand up and sing with joy:

> *"Oh, happy day that fixed my choice*
> *On Thee, my Saviour and my God,*
> *Well may this glowing heart rejoice,*
> *And tell its raptures all abroad."*

> *"He taught me how to watch and pray,*
> *And live rejoicing every day,*
> *Happy day, happy day,*
> *When Jesus washed my sins away."*

There's also a song for those in the full vigor of
the Christian life:

> *"Oh could I speak the matchless worth,*
> *Oh could I sound the glories forth*
> *Which in my Savior shine,*

> *I'd soar, and touch the heav'nly strings,*
> *And vie with Gabriel while he sings*
> *In notes almost divine."*

The Christian also has a song for the hour of sorrow:

> *"When peace, like a river, attendeth my way,*
> *When sorrows like sea billows roll;*
> *Whatever my lot, Thou hast taught me to say,*
> *It is well, it is well, with my soul."*

Or perhaps, comfortingly, he sings:

> *"I must tell Jesus all of my troubles,*
> *I cannot bear these burdens alone,*
> *In my distress He surely will help me,*
> *He ever loves and cares for His own."*

One remembers that Jesus sang in the Upper Room on the night before He was crucified, when the awful burden of the world's sin was upon Him, when the hatred of the race was about to be foisted upon His innocent head, He sang praises unto God at the Passover Feast.

The children of God have a song even in the black hour of death; and you may hear them singing:

> *"Safe in the arms of Jesus,*
> *Safe on His gentle breast,*
> *There by His love o'ershaded,*
> *Sweetly my soul shall rest.*
> *Hark! 'Tis the voice of angels,*

Borne in a song to me,
Over the fields of glory,
Over the jasper sea.
Safe in the arms of Jesus,
Safe on His gentle breast,
There by His love o'ershaded,
Sweetly my soul shall rest."

How true it is that "stone walls do not a prison make, nor iron bars a cage"! Truly our God supplies for those who trust Him "songs in the night."

You know the devil is a fool to persecute God's children; he always loses out when he does. I sometimes think he does not use that technique so often, to-day; rather he lulls them to sleep with indifference. A little persecution would be a mighty good thing for the Church. It would rouse the real Christians and drive out the pretenders. That jail at Philippi became a veritable sanctuary of God. All the saved of the Lord have a song, and they sing it best under pressure and persecution.

IV. CHRISTIANITY IS A RELIGION OF POWER.

There is something more than mere drama about the earthquake. It was undoubtedly a miraculous thing; it may have had its roots in nature, but it had the finger of God directing it, and perhaps it was sent to teach God's power to break the shackles of sin, for we read that, when the earthquake came, the doors were opened and the chains of the prisoners were unloosed.

But Jesus can break every fetter without the help of an earthquake.

> *"He breaks the bonds of cancelled sin,*
> *He sets the prisoner free!"*

Now earthquakes are signs of God's judgment, and since the turn of the century earthquakes have been tremendously on the increase. Records show that a half-million people have been killed—two hundred thousand at one time in China, in 1920. There was an earthquake at the Cross, there was another at the Resurrection, and there will be another great earthquake at the Second Coming of our Lord; but what you need, my friend, if you are outside of Jesus Christ, is a real earthquake in your soul. That's what the Philippian jailer got, and the man who has had an earthquake in his soul by the grace and power of God does not fear the coming judgment because there is no condemnation for him.

If we are ever to have another revival, we must have the power of God come upon the church of Jesus Christ. If that power comes, it will probably come by the way of persecution that brings men low before God and causes them to pray with great earnestness. Then God's power will fall, evil will be defeated, God will be glorified in the salvation of precious souls.

V. CHRISTIANITY IS A RELIGION OF DELIVERANCE.

When the jailer discovered the prison doors open, and the prisoners free, he was about to commit suicide. Hard and relentless Rome would have held him responsible for the safe-keeping of his prisoners, and if they escaped he would likely be put to death.

But he hears Paul's reassuring words: "Do thyself no harm for we are all here." Then, trembling, the jailer asks: "What must I do to be saved?" or, literally, "What must I do to be delivered?"

We doubt that this jailer had any truly evangelical ideas when he asked the question. Fear of physical calamity mingled with a desire for some supernatural deliverance seemed to be uppermost in his mind, but the important thing is that Paul was "quick on the trigger," and used the occasion for the Gospel of Jesus Christ. If the child of God and personal worker is alert, he does not need to wait for an evangelical question to give a gospel answer. Almost any type of conversation can be turned into gospel channels if God's child is seeking to do so.

"What must I do to be saved?" It is a great question, and how variedly it would be answered today. If the Moralist were asked the question, his answer would be, "Be good and trust that God is good, and He will honor your goodness." If a Theosophist were asked, he would give you some vague teaching on the transmigration of souls, and would tell you that your salvation depended upon the upward tendency in these reincarnations and transmigrations. If the Buddhist were asked, he would give you a moral code and a philosophy of life that would end up in Nirvana or the soul's nothingness. Your salvation would come through your ultimate submersion into universal spirit. Ask the Eddyite, or Christian Scientist, falsely so called, and your answer would be that you do not need any salvation except from error. Sin is non-existent, evil is an error of mortal mind, God is all, God is love, God is good. And if you listened long enough, your mind would be hypnotized by this ethereal philosophy.

And what is Paul's answer? It is: "Believe, believe, believe, on the Lord Jesus Christ, and thou shalt be saved." And what does that mean? It means, commit your all to the finished work of Jesus Christ; it means, to confess with your mouth the Lord Jesus, believing in your heart that God hath raised Him from the dead. It means, receiving Him as your personal Saviour, and receiving the authority to become a child of God.

I can scarcely understand how it could be so, but somehow by God's grace that Jailer believed and was saved. Think of it! A raw pagan found Jesus that night in the midst of turmoil, and you who have heard the Gospel all your life say you don't understand the working of it. Ah, beloved, it's not the trouble of your heads but with your hearts; it's not that you don't understand so much as that you are not willing to believe.

The story is told of a prodigal young man of high Russian family in the days of the Czars, who was jailed for his spendthrift habits that had brought him into severe debt. In the prison, in a spirit of remorse, he made a list of his remembered debts, and they totaled a staggering sum. In desperation he wrote absent-mindedly on the paper, "And who will pay these debts?" Exhausted in mind and body, he fell asleep with his arms on the table, the paper in front of him. While he was asleep, Czar Nicholas, who knew the family and the lad, came to the jail and looking in saw the paper and wrote under the statement, "And who will pay these debts?" in a bold hand: "I, Nicholas!" and tiptoed out, while the young man slept on.

Imagine the surprise of the lad when he awoke and saw this statement, and was told of its authenticity and that freedom had been obtained for him. But, oh, what is that compared with the joy of the lost sinner brought face to face with the realization that though his sins were as scarlet, yet by the death of Jesus Christ, they had been made as white as snow. Though the wages of sin were death, yet the gift of God is eternal life through Jesus Christ Our Lord. "Oh, believe it!" says the Apostle. "Believe it!" is my plea to you.

Alexander Maclaren tells the story of an old Rabbi who used to say to his congregation, "Repent the day before you die." But one said to him, "Rabbi, we do not know the day on which we shall die. How then shall we repent the day before?" And the Rabbi replied, with a twinkle in his eye, yet in all seriousness: "Then, repent today." Now is the accepted time—now is the day of salvation.

"Why do you linger, why do you stay,
In the broad road, that most dangerous way—

While right before you, narrow and strait,
Is the bright pathway to heaven's pearly gate?

Come, then, beloved, no longer stay;
Leave the broad highway, oh, leave it to-day!
Make your decision—oh, do not wait!
Take thou the pathway so narrow and strait!"

VII.

THE CONVERSION OF APOLLOS

Acts 10: 24-28.

The Study

The Occasion.

Ephesus, a strategic Greek city, is being evangelized. Priscilla and Aquila, Paul's fellow laborers, are there, evidently doing a great work in the synagogue when Apollos, a preacher from the cultured city of Alexandria in North Africa, puts in his appearance. He speaks in the synagogue and Priscilla and Aquila hear him, and recognize his limited Gospel knowledge.

We are told that Apollos knew only "the baptism of John," which was the Jewish gospel of repentance. And it would appear that he was still preaching the message that John preached. That message was definitely one of Jewish preparation for the coming Messiah. The cry of the Baptist was, "Prepare ye the way of the Lord."

But, in the meantime, Jesus had come, lived, died, risen, and ascended to heaven. According to promise, the Holy Spirit had come at Pentecost and a new dispensation had been ushered in. But Apollos has no awareness of this new revelation and responsibility.

Aquila and Priscilla take Apollos home with them

107

and teach him the truth concerning the Christian Gospel. He then goes forth fired with enthusiasm for the full Gospel message.

The Subject.

Apollos, a Jew of Alexandria, a learned and eloquent man, who, through the Scriptures and the ministry of John the Baptist, became a believer in the coming of Christ, visited Ephesus about A. D. 54. His character seems to be not unlike that of Paul. After his conversion to the Christian gospel he preached with great power and success, especially among the Jews.

The Agent.

Aquila is a Jew born in Pontus, a tentmaker by occupation, who with Priscilla, his wife, joined the Christian Church at Rome. When the Jews were banished from that city by the Emperor Claudius, Aquila and his wife retired to Corinth. They afterwards became companions of Paul in his labors, and are mentioned by him with much commendation, being found both at Ephesus and at Rome. They appear to be devout and patient servants of God and personal workers.

The Accompaniment.

Here is another quiet conversion, though we do not know the conversation and discussion that may have taken place in the Aquilian home.

Results.

A mighty preacher of the Gospel, Apollos becomes effective in a great evangelizing movement through his knowledge of Jesus Christ as Saviour and Lord.

Significant Lessons.

Lots of earnest preachers neither know or preach the true Gospel. The pre-crucifixion message, commonly called "the Jesus way of life," which is so popular to-day, is not "the gospel of the grace of God." Christianity is a post-crucifixion, post-resurrection, post-pentecost message; it is not the religion *of* Jesus but the religion *about* Jesus. Learning and earnestness are no guarantee of truth. No one should be received into the church and its membership on religious knowledge alone. All should know Christ, and know Him experientially. How terrible to go to hell through the Church! Priscilla and Aquila didn't scold the preacher, they taught him. Criticism is a sort of spiritual surgery, and when the operation is performed, the knife must be bathed in love and rendered sterile by the Holy Ghost.

THE SERMON

THE CONVERSION OF A PREACHER

Acts 18: 24-28.

IN OUR study of these "Seven Saved Sinners"— God's varieties of religious experiences, we have considered the conversion of the Ethiopian Eunuch; Cornelius, the Gentile; Saul, the persecutor; Sergius Paulus, the Roman proconsul; Lydia, the business woman of Thyatira, and the Philippian jailer. All of them have been interesting individuals whose peculiar conditions God met through the Gospel and who were gloriously saved.

We come now to one of the most unusual cases—

the conversion of Apollos, an Alexandrian Jew, cultured, fervent, eloquent, and valiant, yet pitifully limited because he knew only the baptism of John. That meant that he had probably heard John the Baptist preach his mighty message concerning the way of the Lord, making straight in the desert a highway for our God. John, as you remember, was forerunner of the Messiah, the Lord Jesus Christ. John baptized those who repented of their sin in preparation for the coming of the Lord. Many who heard John and were converted to righteous living went out and proclaimed the message that he was proclaiming; and apparently Apollos was one of these.

But this was not the message of salvation! In the meantime, Jesus the Messiah had been introduced to Israel. He had gone about doing good, healing and teaching; finally he had been despised and rejected of men and nailed to the cross for the world's redemption. He had risen again from the dead, appeared to the disciples, had given them the apostolic commission, "Go ye into all the world and preach the Gospel to every creature," and had ascended into heaven, telling them to tarry at Jerusalem until they should be endued with power. The Holy Spirit had come on the day of Pentecost. But none of these things did Apollos know, though he was mighty in the Scriptures, preaching what he knew with fervency and with power. Apollos, like many to-day, was a half-Christian, and a half-Christian is in reality no Christian at all.

Yet Apollos was true to all the light he had, and what is more important, he was willing to get more light, and when the devout Christians, Aquila and Priscilla, took him in hand, told him the things that he had not learned, apparently he was an apt pupil and received the Lord Jesus Christ as his personal Saviour, and went forth with renewed power in the preaching of the full gospel of Jesus Christ.

I. APOLLOS IS A TYPE OF A GREAT GROUP OF UNSAVED PREACHERS.

It is with sorrow of heart that I am forced to declare that many men in the pulpits, to-day, have no saving knowledge of Jesus Christ, and, while they are pretending to help others to heaven, they are not going there themselves.

Some are deceived about the faith, having never been to the Cross of Jesus Christ. So many are preaching a pre-crucifixion message. Some years ago a noted educator, who was then the editor of a rather famous religious magazine, came out and declared that what the world needed was a propagation of the religion *of* Jesus instead of a religion *about* Jesus. Our liberal friends took up the cry, and we have had a great deal of propagating of the gospel they call "the Jesus way of life." Its chief message is the Sermon on the Mount, the ethics and example of Jesus. The Cross is backgrounded and becomes an incident, or an accident, in the life of a Great Teacher.

Now, we do not despise the pre-crucifixion and pre-resurrection message of Jesus, but Christianity is a post-crucifixion, post-resurrection, and post-pentecostal message. The religion of Jesus was a sort of glorified

Judaism. The religion of Christianity is a religion not *of* Jesus but *about* Jesus.

If you will study the Gospels carefully, you will see that the Cross is the turning point. There were no real Christians before the Cross. John was not a Christian in the modern sense, neither was Peter. There are vastly too many people hiding behind Peter's vacillating personality before Pentecost. But don't look at Peter before he was baptized in the Spirit, but afterwards, and I'll guarantee he'll be a challenge to your life. In reality, Peter was *not* a Christian before Pentecost. He was simply a good Jew who was following Jesus as the Messiah.

Even Jesus was not a Christian. As a man He was a Jew. He was made of a woman—made under the law. He kept the law and was faithful to the ceremonies and to the sacrifices. Christ was not a Christian, *but Christianity is Christ.* Paul gives his definition when he says: "I am crucified with Christ, nevertheless I live, yet not I, but Christ liveth in me, and the life which I now live in the flesh I live by the faith of the Son of God, who loved me and gave himself for me." Christianity is not primarily a creed. It is not a code of ethics or moral laws. Christianity is a supernatural life. It is Jesus Christ, redeemed and indwelling the human soul. Every born-again Christian can truly say, for me to live is Christ. It is not the life of Jesus that the Christian glories in, but the death of Jesus, and He says with the Apostle, "God forbid that I should glory save in the cross of our Lord Jesus Christ by which the world is crucified unto me and I unto the world." And with the poet he sings:

"In the Cross of Christ I glory,
Towering o'er the wrecks of time,
All the light of sacred story
Gathers round its head sublime.

When the woes of life o'ertake me,
Hopes deceive and fears annoy,
Never shall the Cross forsake me,
Lo, it glows with peace and joy."

Apollos would have made a first-class liberal as he was. Thank God, when he was converted through faith in Jesus Christ, he became a first-class Christian and Gospel preacher!

Others, through apostasy, deny the faith. Again I am sorrowful in declaring that I believe many who occupy the pulpit to-day are "angels of light" and servants of the evil one. For you know the devil has become an angel of light and his ministers, ministers of righteousness. The devil is a religionist, as we have already noted. He has ministers; and some of them occupy prominent pulpits.

If this *statement* startles you, let me give you some illustrations. Take, for example, a prominent New York minister who in the book he published, some years ago, declared subtly against the resurrection of the Lord Jesus by saying: "I believe in the immortality of the soul, but not in the resurrection of the flesh." Now the apostle Paul says, "If there be no resurrection of the flesh, then is Christ not risen, and, if Christ be not risen, then is our preaching vain and we are yet in our sins, and they who have fallen asleep in Jesus have perished!"

Do not be deceived, no man is a Christian who does not believe in the physical resurrection of Jesus Christ, for the Word of God says, "That if thou shalt confess with thy mouth the Lord Jesus, believing in thine heart that God hath raised him from the dead, thou shalt be saved." No man who denies the resurrection of Jesus can ever be saved.

This same author says, again: "The Master's body was like ours. He suffered and died like ourselves. Away with your theological Christ; give us an ethical leader." Harsh and unfeeling as it may sound, I declare that such a man needs to be saved.

A Baptist theological professor in a book dealing with the modernistic message, declares, in a chapter entitled "The Religion of Salvation," that the idea of inherited guilt from Adam is laughable. "One has only to state such a view to see how remote it is from the present day thought about wrong doing." I remember as I read that book I looked all through the chapter that was supposed to deal with salvation and found no mention of the Cross, and only in the next chapter is it spoken of, and then to ridicule its message.

Another local clergyman, writing in *Harper's Magazine*, on the subject, "The Vanishing Sinner," says: "What is right in one generation is wrong in another, and *vice versa*. The delineation of sin has thus undergone a transition," he declares, "somewhat similar to that which has taken place in painting. The old clear-cut lines have given way to an impressionistic indefiniteness. The black and white contrasts to low-toned greys. In this the Church officially has played a part, not only for the reasons mentioned above, but for another which Prof. Coe has recently brought forth most potently. He says the Church has lightened the old darkness of natural depravity, because it cannot by contrast demonstrate an actuality of regeneration. The so-called Protestant conversions do not reveal a sufficient distinctive righteousness in our industrial order for observers to identify them as redeemed."

We realize the Gospel that these men preach would not create distinctive Christians. But whence comes the audacity of these men to deny that the Gospel of Jesus Christ preached fearlessly by faithful men of God through the centuries has created distinctive and unmistakable Christians with the righteousness of God? What shall they say to the conversion of Jerry McAuley, the river rat? What of Valentine Burke, the jewel thief? What of Mel Trotter? What of Billy Sunday? What of a million others whose feet have been lifted from the miry clay and placed upon the solid rock, into whose mouth the song of salvation has been placed, even praises unto God, and whose lives have testified to the power of the Gospel of Jesus Christ? I declare these men need to be saved themselves, and to know Jesus experimentally.

II. APOLLOS IS A TYPE OF CHURCH MEMBER WHO JOINS
    THE CHURCH UPON EARLY RELIGIOUS TRAINING.

There are many of these, and I trust I may waken
some of them out of their deadly slumber. These are
the children of devout Christians who have been brought
up in the warm atmosphere of a Christian home, and
who have never doubted the doctrinal realities of the
Christian faith, and somehow or other they think that
they are saved because they believe as their mother
did, and have never denied their father's religion.

But saving faith does not come by heredity. Thank
God for the children of Christian parents! What would
some of us do had it not been for praying mothers?
We could not sing as we do:

> *"I grieved my Lord from day to day,*
> *I spurned His love so full and free,*
> *And though I wandered far away,*
> *Yet mother's prayers have followed me."*

It is well to remember that none of us can go to
heaven on our mother's religion! We must have an
experience of our own, definite, clear, and unmistakable! Then there are others among this group who somehow or other feel that they are saved by religious
knowledge. They have learned the catechism, they have
been through confirmation, they have had their salvation passed on to them supposedly by the hands of a
minister or a priest, and they have a certificate to that
end, and that's all that they have.

A friend of mine, dealing with a woman in the

city of Chicago, asking her about her salvation, heard her say that she could prove that she was saved by the confirmation certificate she had. She went upstairs to find it—the meeting was being held on the street— and after she was gone for considerable time, she came down in dismay, declaring that she had put the certificate in the bureau drawer and that the mice had gotten in and eaten it up, and she wasn't sure, because of this, whether she was saved or not! Oh, beloved, know Jesus Christ as your Saviour, and you will have the confirmation of the indwelling presence of the Holy Spirit; that's something mice can't destroy.

Many churches have "Easter hatchings" in which the children especially are all rounded up and received into the membership of the church. It makes a great showing, but when you receive a child into the church and try to burglarize its soul for the sake of a showing, you are doing the cause of Christ a terrible injury and perhaps helping to plunge a soul into eternity without God!

In a certain church of which I was pastor, a girl came to me one night after evening service in tears. She was a church member. "Oh, Mr. Ayer, I've never been saved," she said. "I was taken into the church because the pastor wanted me to become a member and be baptized at Easter-time, as others were coming in, and so I felt it was the right thing to do; but I've never found Jesus." Well, thank God, she *did* find Jesus, and was re-baptized upon her profession of faith.

Many years ago, while a student in Chicago, I was teaching a Sunday School class in a certain church. It

was during the days of the World War, and on the last
day of an evangelistic campaign; the evangelist stood
up on the platform, seeking the decision of the boys
and girls. Taking the flag, which at that time was a
great emotional rallying centre, and holding it beside
the pulpit, he gave this invitation: "How many of you
want to stand for God and country, come forward, and
give me your hand?" Almost all the pupils of the Sunday School went forward on this invitation; then the
evangelist went into spasms of ecstasy, declaring that he
was going to wire on to the next place where he was to
hold a meeting that God had given great victory there in
Chicago, and that practically every soul in the Sunday
School had been brought to Jesus Christ that morning!
Oh, how my heart ached! I hung my head in shame.
What a mockery of the cause of Christ!

But this is but a picture of the condition of thousands who are brought into the church by some such
trick as this in their childhood. They have been taught
to believe in Jesus in a sort of mental way, but they
have not been born again. When they reach adolescence
with the tug and pull of the sinful age upon their
lives, and have no power to hold them, no stability of
spiritual life, they leave the church, they leave the
home, they leave righteousness by the tens of thousands,
and the palaces of pleasure and the pathways of sin
are glutted with these poor deluded souls. Oh, may
God call some of you to salvation through Jesus Christ.
How terrible to pass beneath the pulpit and through
the sacred aisles of God's sanctuary, out into the dark-

ness of eternal separation from God, to hear the Lord Jesus say: "Depart from Me, I never knew you!"

III. APOLLOS, LIKE MANY A CHURCH MEMBER, WAS ZEALOUS FOR WHAT HE KNEW.

We have a number of church workers, to-day, who are zealous but unsaved. They labor in the Missionary Society, and in the Ladies' Aid Society; they labor in the men's work of the church, and yet they know nothing about the saving power of Jesus Christ. Some of them teach Sunday School classes. I know because I've had men and women come to me and say, "Mr. Ayer, I've been teaching a Sunday School class for years, but I do not know Jesus as my personal Saviour, and therefore I have never led one of my pupils to Him." These people are not to be condemned primarily, they are to be pitied. Many of them have never heard the Gospel presented in an uncompromising way. They have a feeling that by their good works they are going to merit heaven. They are faithful to what they believe to be their duty in the kingdom of God, and yet they are utterly deluded.

If you're one of these, let me remind you that you'll not get to heaven the way you're going. I'm reminded of the automobilist traveling along the country highway, who hailed a country lad, asking: "How far to Hilltown, Sonny?" The bright lad with a twinkle in his eye said, "Well, Mister, it's about 24,995 miles the way you're going, but if you'll turn around you'll be there in no time, for it's about five miles in that direction." Remember the word of the Apostle Paul:

"Not by works of righteousness which we have done, but according to His mercy He saved us by the washing of regeneration and the renewing of the Holy Ghost," and "by grace are ye saved through faith and that not of yourselves, it is the gift of God, not of works lest any man should boast."

IV. LIKE MANY A CHURCH MEMBER, APOLLOS NEEDED A PERSONAL EXPERIENCE WITH JESUS CHRIST.

Aquila and Priscilla listened to Apollos and knew that he didn't know the truth. Now, my friend, would *you* know? Are you sufficiently spiritually-minded to discern the Gospel or to notice the absence of it?

Some years ago, at a young people's gathering held in the city in which I was pastor, a speaker got up and talked to a great group of young people from the Mother Goose text: "Simple Simon met a pieman going to the fair." She talked a lot of ethereal nonsense, but when she was through, the young people applauded, and many older people went up and told her it was a marvelous message. One of the reasons why we have modernists in the pulpits is because we have spiritually ignorant people in the pew. *Where God's people know the truth, liberalism does not thrive.*

Now these two conscientious Christians, Priscilla and Aquila, not only knew the sound of the truth when they heard it, but they knew how to deal with a situation such as Apollos presented. Again I ask, would you? It is noticeable that they didn't fight with this man from North Africa, nor did they belittle him. They saw not only his limitations but also his earnestness.

Here is a truth for our hearing and heeding. Our sympathy must go out to some men who occupy pulpits and some Christians who are deluded, because they have never had an opportunity to know. Most of our ministers are the products of the seminaries which they attend, and if the seminaries do not teach them truth, how can we expect our ministers to know it? Perhaps we need to be more patient, but not more indifferent. There are many men standing in Christian pulpits who need our prayers and sympathy. Scolding will do no good. Would you scold a lost child? Would you deride a drowning man? Let our hearts be touched to the quick. God pity them. Many of these men are blind leaders of the blind.

Let us be careful of criticism. It is a most delicate task we have to perform when we are called to perform it. Criticism is a sort of spiritual surgery. What would we think of the surgeon that rushed carelessly into the operating room, and lashed at the patient unmercifully with his scalpel? If God calls us to this task, and He sometimes does, we must have our knives of criticism bathed in love and made sterile by the Holy Ghost.

It is important to note that preachers are especially sensitive about their sermons. They are about as jealous of them as mothers are of their children, but Priscilla and Aquila had the right idea in dealing with the situation.

I can imagine that they worked it this way. Priscilla went up to Apollos after the morning service sweetly and said that she was very glad to have heard him and wished that inasmuch as he was a stranger in town, he might come home with Aquila and herself to dinner. Now they didn't discuss the sermon on the way home, nor did they talk about it at meal time. No preacher should ever be criticized until after he has eaten. It might ruin his digestion!

I can imagine also that it was a wonderful meal that Priscilla prepared. Quite likely there was fried chicken, and sweet potatoes, and corn on the cob, boiled onions and hubbard squash; and then, to top off the meal, a generous slice of pumpkin pie with whipped cream on the top and a good cup of coffee. And by the time Apollos had eaten this glorious repast, he was in an excellent frame of mind. Who wouldn't be?

Then, doubtless, they retired to the parlor and, while Priscilla washed the dishes, Aquila talked with Apollos about many things. He brought the conversation around to the things of the Spirit, and had already told him about the new truth that had come to the world; that there was another and greater message than that which John had preached; that Jesus the Messiah had come, that He had died, and that He rose again, and that He had sent the Holy Ghost. Then Priscilla joined the company and in a kind, motherly way took the young and fiery Apollos to Scripture after Scripture that he well knew, and taught him the things concerning Jesus, the Saviour.

The heart of the young preacher, already touched by their hospitality and kindness, was, through their testimony, touched by the Spirit of the living God. I

don't believe it was hard for them to get him to make
a definite acceptance of Jesus Christ as his personal
Saviour. Then down on their knees they go, Aquila
and Priscilla with their arms about the young preacher,
the tears coursing down their faces, asking God to have
the Lord Jesus come into his heart by the Spirit, to
give him a conscious knowledge of sin forgiven through
the death and resurrection of the Lord Jesus Christ;
to send him forth in a mighty ministry of the Gospel.
When they arose from their knees a new light was shin-
ing in the face of Apollos. He had been born again,
the resurrected Christ was indwelling his heart. Small
wonder that he went forth from that place believing
through grace, to help the disciples of the Lord, preaching in might and power, convincing the Jews, and that
publicly, showing by the Scriptures that Jesus was the
Christ.

This shows the essential humility of the great
Apollos. Not only was he learned, but he was humble;
and, best of all, he received Jesus. Will you? Oh, I
realize how hard it is to make a stand if once you've
professed. It's harder to save a church member than
one who has never made a stand of any kind. Some
one has said that the three hardest words to pronounce,
in the English language, are—"I am wrong."

I have met a goodly number who are in this condition; who have come with heaviness of heart and declared that they did not know Jesus, though they were
church members. I'll never forget a girl in the city
of Valparaiso, Indiana, who declared to me with tears,
"Oh, Mr. Ayer, people think I'm a Christian, but I'm

not. I live a good life, I teach a Sunday School class, but I've never found Jesus and I want to find Him." Well, thank God, she found him that night, for Jesus was seeking her.

On one occasion in the city of Gary, in the same state, I baptized approximately a dozen people who had previously professed Christianity but had never accepted the Lord Jesus as their personal Saviour. Some of them had been baptized into the church, but later found Christ, and now were being re-baptized upon their profession of faith.

Several years later the young lady from Valparaiso, of whom I have spoken, called me by long distance telephone while I was pastor in Gary, and asked me to pray for a certain young man, the son of a deacon in the church in that city. "Mr. Ayer," she said, "he admitted to me some time ago that he was not saved." "Why," I said, "that can't be; I know this young fellow well, I've known him for years. He was active in the B. Y. P. U.—surely he was saved." "No," she replied, "he's in awful misery of soul for he knows he's not a child of God."

My mind went back over the years of contact with that family. I remembered how we visited this young man's home while he was still in high school. I remembered how I officiated at the funeral of his devout Christian mother, and I remembered how this lad, then in the early twenties, had wept so inconsolably at her loss. There was no comforting the boy. I thought it queer for I had tried to tell him that his mother had gone to heaven and that he would see her one day, but he would not be comforted, and now I understood— he had no hope!

So I said to the girl, "Get the lad on the 'phone." "He's out of town," she replied, "I can't reach him." "Well," I said, "write him, tell him to come to see me, and not fail, if he comes to this part of the country." "Oh, Mr. Ayer," the girl went on, "here's the sad thing, he's afraid to talk with you. He's ashamed because he's been professing to be a Christian and he knows that you thought he was saved and a child of God. Oh, pray for him," she cried, as she hung up the receiver.

And I *did* pray, and I continue to pray. I don't know where that lad is to-night, although I've tried to find him. I have never seen him since, to talk with him. And somewhere there's a fine, clean-cut, upstanding lad, whose mother went to heaven, whose father, now an old man, is trusting in Jesus, the majority of whose family are saved and safely in the kingdom, who walks in heaviness of heart, unless he has steeled his conscience against the truth. He has his name on a church book, the majority of the people think he is a child of God because he was a clean-living lad, but this boy will never see that sainted mother unless he yields himself to Jesus Christ. Oh, that I knew where I might find him, and talk with him about Jesus!

But while I'm thinking and talking about him, I am not unmindful that there are thousands of similar cases who are religious but do not know God; who are church members but who have never been saved; who, like Apollos, are living up to the light that they know, but who have not received the full light as it is in Jesus. Oh, may God help you to heed the message that except you repent you will perish, but know, also, that the Lord Jesus is inviting you to salvation, saying, "Whosoever will may come and him that cometh unto me I will in no wise cast out."

> *"Just as thou art, without one trace*
> *Of love, or joy, or inward grace,*
> *Or meetness for the heavenly place,*
>   *O guilty sinner, come!*
>
> *Burdened with guilt, wouldst thou be blest?*
> *Trust not the world, it gives no rest;*
> *Christ brings relief to hearts opprest;*
>   *O weary sinner, come!"*

PRINTED IN THE UNITED STATES OF AMERICA